Starting With Me, Starting Today

Other Books By Bill Sanders

Starting With Me, Starting Today

A Teen Leadership Manual

Bill Sanders

National Character Education Foundation
Zelienople, PA

Starting With Me, Starting Today
by Bill Sanders

Published by:

National Character Education Foundation
300 South Main Street
Zelienople, PA 16063
866-770-6233
631-724-0120 (fax)
www.ncef.net

ISBN-10: 09789553-0-7
ISBN-13: 978-0-978553-0-4

Printed in the United States of America
20 19 18 17 16 15 14 13 12 11 10 9 8 7 6 5 4 3 2 1

This book is dedicated to my three children, Emily, Crystal and Brandon. I wish every young person reading this book could know you three and model their lives after you. Your mom and I are so proud of the integrity you live by, the compassion you have always shown others and the goals you are setting and reaching daily.

Acknowledgements

This book came about "for such a time as this". I thought I was at a point in my career when my book writing days were coming to an end. That is, until I met Dave Rettig, the founder of The National Character Education Foundation (NCEF). Talk about energy and drive. He has it. Just being near Dave, one can't help but feel a deep concern for the tough times in which our nation's children live, and hence, the desperate need for equipping them with long lost character skills. Thanks Dave for embracing me, encouraging me, caring for me, and being a great friend. I hope you find this book a fitting reflection of what our young people need in the way of building them up from the inside out with honesty, integrity, and hope.

The staff at NCEF have become like family to me. They are dedicated day in and day out with no fanfare or headlines. While we are out speaking to a group of students, getting our fix, they plod along with never-ending concern for the youth of America. Dorothy, you are an amazing person with so much to offer. Jean, your smile and enthusiasm come across on the phone each time I am blessed to talk with you. Bob, without your organizational skills we might be making better time, but we would surely be going in the wrong direction.

Holly, my wonderful wife of 31 years, you are an eternal source of both understanding and encouragement to keep on keeping on, no matter how many days I may be in the road yacking away. Of course, we have always said around our house that it really is best for everyone if dad (me) leaves for a few days each week to give advice to someone else.

Special thanks goes to Brandon Sanders and Jim Wooden for all of your efforts on putting together the cover design.

The good Lord has once again orchestrated this new chapter in my life, and as always I am very grateful...

Table of Contents

Introduction

It starts with you...

What would cause an entire football team to have so much compassion and love for a fellow student who had lost his hair to leukemia, that they would shave their heads so he wouldn't feel alone and out of place? Sure, they could have chosen to fight the students who were calling their friend names like "cue ball", "baldy", and "onion head", but instead they decided to *start with themselves* and live by the Golden Rule.

Why would one junior high girl have the courage to sit next to the most feared and despised bully the school had ever known? Why would she become his friend when no one else would have anything to do with him? More importantly, why would she want to stand out from her friends and be nice to the guy who beat up her brother the day before? It's because she believed that courage *started with her* and it *started that day*!

How could a guy with no right hand go on to make the high school, college, and major league baseball teams as a pitcher, and against all odds, throw a no-hitter for the New York Yankees? With less natural ability than hundreds of previous big league pitchers, and only half the required number of hands, what kind of determination, drive, and desire caused this likable young man to act so differently from so many others striving for this most cherished and elusive goal? It's simple: he believed that persistence and determination *started with him* day by day.

Why would one of the most famous speakers of all time invite dozens of other speakers to his organization to give away his secrets on how to reach teens? On top of that, why would he personally help the speakers get to their rooms by carrying their bags? When I asked him why he seemed so full of pleasure in serving us, he said: "My hero washed feet." Serving others for the good of teenagers **started with him, starting that day**.

How could a woman who had just left her husband's funeral find the compassion to go to the house of the teenage boy who had accidentally hit him with a car to tell him that not only would everything be OK, but that he should forgive himself so his life wouldn't be ruined? What special quality did she possess inside that would cause her to be so different from other angry and resentful people, and in the process, give a young man the freedom to live? For her, setting a good example and caring for others **started with her**, and it **started that day**.

What would cause some professional athletes to not only say no to the pressures of premarital sex in an age when "everybody who is anybody is doing it", but to start an organization called "Athletes for Abstinence"? With plenty of available females at every turn, and so many other sports stars taking advantage of them, what causes some superstars to stand out and stick to their morals? To them, integrity and being able to look yourself in the mirror and like what you see **started with them** and it had to be lived out day by day.

What would drive a sixth-grader to act independently from all his other classmates and gather enough signatures to encourage the state of Ohio to adopt its new motto: "All things are possible with God"? He believed **every decision counts and everybody matters**.

Why would a nun give up fame and fortune to serve this world's downtrodden? When her picture gets on the cover of nationally known magazines and they tell her inspiring stories, what causes her to live out her faith and not care for the spotlight? She believed being authentic and not a hypocrite **started with her** if she would have any real impact on the world.

Being a leader who says, *"starting with me, starting today"* is what this book is all about. The secrets of the people you have just read about, and dozens more, are awaiting you in the pages ahead. You'll learn how to become the type of person you will be proud of walking down the hall of your school. I'm talking about real, live, hard-to-find, positive leadership -- the stuff heroes are made of. I want you to become the kind of leader you don't read much about anymore -- not a manipulative, self-serving, dictator-type leader, but the kind of leader we all admire.

The world is ready for you and all that you have to offer. You have what it takes! I know that without even personally knowing you. I can say that with confidence because I've been studying leaders for over twenty years. They come in all shapes, sizes, and backgrounds. You need to understand that you have been created for greatness, and designed to show the world your greatness. By following the step-by-step techniques in this book you can -- and will -- better yourself, and find that you can fulfill the unique dreams that you were meant to achieve.

I have answered over 15 thousand letters in the last 25 years from people of all ages, especially teens. Many of these people are trying desperately to figure out what makes some people successful and some people miserable. Starting With Me, Starting Today is filled with simple, yet seldom-used, principles that can help you be the kind of integrity-filled person our world is trying so hard to find. All you have to do is learn the principles and apply them. In order to do that you must read on, and put into practice what you learn. **Everybody matters and every decision counts, starting with you, starting today!**

This book is meant to be written in, underlined, and used. If you merely read it and put no more effort into it than that, please don't expect great things to happen. This is your teen survival manual! It is to be referred to over and over again.

Note: There are no right or wrong answers to the questions asked in this book. What's important is for you to learn to express yourself and find out that your thoughts are worthwhile and important. If you don't believe in yourself, few others will either.

1 Someone Believes In You

"You must be the change you see in the world."
– *Mahatma Gandhi, pacifist*

If you have been chosen to be a part of your school's Leadership Program, "Starting with Me, Starting Today", please read the following carefully and answer the questions. If you are reading this book on your own, realize that you too have special people in your life who see your true potential and want the best for you.

Someone believes in you.
Someone sees you as a positive leader.
Someone voted for you to be here today.
Someone sees potential in you.
Someone thinks you are capable of more.
Someone feels you are destined for great things.
Someone can picture you being a positive force in
　　　this school.
Someone believes the time and energy invested in
　　　you will be worthwhile.
Someone has faith in you.
Someone is willing to put their name and
　　　reputation on the line for you.
Someone has the foresight to look beyond who you
　　　are now to what you can become.
Someone sees qualities of himself/herself in you.
Someone has your best interest in mind.
Someone has a gut feeling that you can put forth
　　　the effort needed to help change your
　　　school.

Q: Why are you reading this book?
A: Someone believes in you.
A: You have real leadership potential
A: You are investing in yourself.

1

Someone cares enough about your future to invest in you.

Someone knows you have what it takes to reach students with no hope.

Someone can picture you putting forth the effort and discipline needed to stick with this program throughout the school year.

Throughout this book you will be asked to write your answers down. You can write them in the space provided, and write in the margins too, if you need more room.

Q: How do you feel, knowing that a teacher or student chose you to be a part of this group because they believe in you?

Q: Does it motivate you to want to be a better person knowing that others are behind you?

Q: Is this a new feeling for you, or have you had others in your life pull for you and encourage you to live up to your potential?

What Character Qualities do Leaders Possess?

Hint: Think of the qualities you value in a friend

- Character qualities are things you work for.
- You earn them by the decisions you make and the promises you keep.
- They have more to do with your reputation than your popularity.
- Character qualities are things that each and every one of us can capture if we are willing to put forth the effort and live them out.

111 Character Qualities of Leaders/Mentors:

1. Honesty
2. Integrity
3. People skills
4. Hard working
5. Good listener
6. Cares for others
7. Makes good eye contact
8. Organized
9. Does what is right even if it isn't popular
10. Isn't afraid of making decisions
11. Looks out for those less fortunate
12. Pulls for the underdog
13. Does random acts of kindness as a way of life
14. Gives sincere compliments
15. Pleasing personality
16. Respectful of everyone
17. Keeps promises
18. Tells the truth
19. Avoids gossip
20. Doesn't laugh at off-color or sexual jokes
21. Has confidence
22. Avoids destructive behaviors
23. Hard worker
24. Never uses people for personal gain
25. Believe the best about others
26. Thinks more in the "we" than the "me"
27. Isn't afraid to sit next to an unpopular student

Character Qualities are different than looks, popularity, wealth, family, intelligence, coordination, weight, and height.

28. Is usually the first to pick up someone's books if they drop them
29. Respects his/her family
30. Does his/her share in making his/her family better
31. Doesn't take his/her parents or family for granted
32. Is thankful for all of his/her blessings and skills
33. Believes in being on time
34. Contented
35. Hopeful
36. Kind to animals
37. Refuses to laugh at others
38. Is a big enough person to say please, thank you, I'm sorry, and please forgive me
39. Has confidence when facing a challenge
40. Has vision for his/her future and the future of his/her school
41. Cares about his/her community
42. Is willing to learn what he/she doesn't know about any subject
43. Sees the best in others
44. Motivates others to do their best
45. Is a person of wisdom
46. Has courage, and will fight for what is right
47. People seek him/her out because of his/her listening skills
48. Takes responsibility for himself/herself
49. Has pride in his/her studying ability
50. Has a good sense of humor
51. Can laugh at himself/herself
52. Avoids sarcasm
53. Looks for solutions to problems
54. Takes time out for himself/herself
55. Gets plenty of sleep
56. Exercises regularly
57. Eats healthy foods
58. Obeys the law
59. Respects authority
60. Honors the person he/she is dating
61. Chooses what to watch and listen to
62. Has self-discipline
63. Knows where he/she wants to go in life

64. Knows each decision he/she make affects the rest of his/her life
65. Communicates clearly in a group setting
66. Never dominates a conversation
67. Encourages others to give their opinion
68. Respects other people's opinion, even if opposed to it
69. Is willing to change in areas where he/she is wrong or needs improvement
70. Listens to older, wiser people on a regular basis
71. Puts effort into his/her spiritual life
72. Earns the trust of others by his/her actions and follow-through
73. Gives feedback to others
74. Builds enthusiasm in others, as well as ideas
75. Gets involved with ideas no matter how much work is involved
76. Has a servant's heart
77. Puts others first
78. Is a good role model
79. Is interested enough in others to learn their names
80. Has high ethics
81. Is willing to take risks if they believe in something
82. Is willing to admit mistakes
83. Respects substitute teachers
84. Speaks ill will of no one
85. Looks at the facts before drawing conclusions
86. Doesn't judge others
87. Considers others' points of view
88. Is willing to mentor and coach others
89. Keeps promises
90. Follows through on commitments
91. Is teachable, available, and trustworthy
92. Walks his/her talk
93. Seeks first to understand rather than to be understood
94. Sets goals for himself/herself and his/her school
95. Optimistic about almost everything
96. Knows own strengths and weaknesses
97. Self-motivated
98. Able to say no

*Starting today you can work on each of these **character qualities** and make them party of your life.*

5

99. Has a purpose in life
100. Adaptable
101. Determined to succeed
102. Flexible
103. Respects self and others
104. Trustworthy
105. Trusting
106. Friendly, forgiving, fun to be around
107. Believes kindness is cool
108. Inquisitive
109. Energetic
110. Overcomes setbacks
111. Believes in delayed gratification

Look over the above list, and write down five character qualities you already have and live by:

1. _____
2. _____
3. _____
4. _____
5. _____

Now write five qualities from the list that you are going to work on in the next few weeks before we meet again as a group:

1. _____
2. _____
3. _____
4. _____
5. _____

Whenever you are in a group setting and discussing ideas and leadership thoughts, keep these key points in mind:

Things said in the group setting should be kept confidential.

- Everyone is to be respected by everyone else. When someone is talking, we ask that everyone else listens carefully and tries to make good eye contact.

- Put your best effort forth today. When it's time to write down your thoughts, do it. Respect your own thoughts and ideas, and write and share them with confidence.

- The single greatest communication skill that will be needed during this session is LISTENING. We have a lot to do and your time is valuable, so listen and follow directions the best you can. I know this will be a great experience for everyone.

Now let's form a plan of action to help you improve in these 5 areas. For each of the 5 items, write down 3 practical steps that you are going to do to instill these character qualities into your life.

Before our next meeting, your leadership assignment is to rewrite both the 5 character qualities that you intend to work on and the 3 steps that will help you obtain each of these qualities. You will be asked to share these steps, and how you feel you are doing in these areas, at our next meeting.

For instance, if the first quality you chose from the list is "Being nice to others", you could do these 3 things to gain this skill:

Example:
1. Being nice to others
A. Offer to help someone with a heavy load.
B. Say thank you to the food service people each day in the cafeteria.
C. Start by being nicer at home.

1. _____
A. _____
B. _____
C. _____

2. _____
A. _____
B. _____
C. _____

3. _____
A. _____
B. _____
C. _____

4. _____
A. _____
B. _____
C. _____

5. _____
A. _____
B. _____
C. _____

2 Fame Is Impressive
(but it isn't leadership)

"The single most important and irresistible question is, what are you doing for someone else."
– Martin Luther King Jr.

Leadership! What's That?
Popularity... everyone wants it, and many people pay a heavy price for it. How important is it to you? It almost ruined me as a teen. I followed the wrong crowd, did many of the wrong things, and have bad memories to prove it. I don't want that for you. I want you to realize that being popular and being a leader are two different things.

The winners of American Idol are popular and famous and have great talent, but unless I know their character, I cann't really call them leaders. Nor would I want you or me to act like them and follow in their footsteps.

Separating Fame from Leadership

Several years ago, Charles Barkley, the Phoenix Suns basketball player, said, "I'm not a role model; I'm a basketball player." He has a clear picture of the difference between leading and being in the newspapers, and I think it's good he does. His physical prowess on the court helped him lead his team to victory, but young people should watch out before they decide to follow his lifestyle. He may be famous, but I think it's good that he doesn't hold himself up for others to follow.

Tiger Woods, Michael Jordan, Derik Jeter, and Lance Armstrong are famous and popular as well; but they are also leaders. They are admired not only for the talent and hard work ethic they live by, but for the good things they do for others away from their respective sports.

9

Fame is impressive, but it isn't leadership, because leaders are people of whom we can say, "I want to be like him," or "I'd be proud to have the character qualities that everyone can see in her life." How many famous people can you honestly say that about?

Just because someone is popular, you can't assume he or she will be a good role model. You won't want to build your life on everything famous people do or say.

Let's also look at the flip side. Does being a leader mean you will become famous? If you become a leader, will you make the news and have newscasters clamoring to interview you? Not necessarily. Real leaders may never live a glamorous lifestyle; the "good life" may escape them. Why? Because fame and fortune are not what real leadership is all about. Leadership is about character -- being able to look at yourself in the mirror and feel proud of the things you see. It's about taking a stand for what you know is right, even if it won't make you popular.

If you have doubts about the truth of that, ask yourself the following questions about the two famous leaders, Martin Luther King Jr. and Abraham Lincoln:

Did they have an easy life?

Were they always famous and popular?

Did they have to fight for what they believed in?

What was the final price they paid?

Neither of these leaders had an easy time of it. When he made his now-famous speech in Washington, D.C., Dr. King had not attracted much fame and popularity. He suffered a lot for his stand. Only today can we admire him easily -- from the distance time has brought. President Lincoln fought to end slavery, earning himself many enemies along the way. Even when he was in the White House, many made fun of him and his policies. Ultimately, both men died by assassins' bullets.

Sure, some people may earn fleeting fame for things that did not require the kind of sacrifice Lincoln and King made. But will anyone remember what these people have done a hundred years from now, as we remember Lincoln? Will they have changed the course of history, like King? And if they are remembered, will they be in the same class as these two men? It's not likely. Fame is impressive, but it isn't leadership.

Leadership Quiz

Ask yourself the following questions.

How much do fame and popularity have to do with leadership?

Don't leaders all have the good life at their fingertips?

Can you be famous and not be a leader?

Can you be a leader and not be famous?

3 The Cost of Leading

"The battles that count aren't the ones for gold medals. The struggles within yourself – the invisible, inevitable battles inside all of us – that's where it's at."
– Jesse Owens, athlete

Why would anyone want to be a leader? I asked myself that question when I started writing this book. After all, it probably takes about five times as much integrity to be a leader as it does sitting back and going with the flow. It also takes enthusiasm and character; and these qualities don't always come easily.

Leadership that counts isn't a cakewalk. To achieve anything of lasting importance, you'll pay a price. So let's start counting the cost.

Sacrifice

The number one character trait that best describes what it takes to lead is servanthood. People who lead -- really lead -- put themselves out for others, even when it's uncomfortable. They put themselves on the line for the good of others. They will, in other words, sacrifice when they need to.

Most people don't find the idea of servanthood or sacrifice either glamorous or exciting. They'd rather have a fancy home than see that someone in need has housing. They'd rather get on the evening news than serve the people who elected them by protecting and fighting for them in Congress. How many of our leaders do you think would still serve if it meant they would never get the fame?

Time

Effective leadership will cost you time. You'll have to put forth effort, even though it does not feel comfortable, and you may want to spend your time elsewhere. Anything less

13

Q: In what area of your life could you be a better servant?

Q: In what ways could you be less selfish and sacrifice some of the time you would normally spend on yourself to better think of others first? (write out answers for each)

At home:

At school:

With your friends:

With students you don't know but see often:

will not create the kind of leadership that changes lives. For example, if I have to write another book or prepare a speech, I must spend a lot of time in a quiet place, grinding out the words and ideas. That means I can't spend as much time with others -- and I like to spend time with people!

Once I've prepared the speech, I get to do the fun part. As I'm standing in front of hundreds of people, about to share my ideas, I finally start to feel the enthusiasm; adrenaline flows through my body, and it feels exciting. I get to at last see some of the results of my work when people tell me how my words changed their lives, caused them to think, or challenged them.

Yet, I wouldn't have much to say, and I wouldn't influence many people, if I never spent that lonely time writing my ideas out. In fact, there are many days, after I get up early and have my quiet time, when part of me would rather be playing a game of tennis, watching TV, calling a friend, playing cards, or doing a host of other things. Following my feelings would be easy, but it would never make me a leader. Emotionally, I would much rather invest my time early each day on ways that give me the best chance of living the way I desire; but doing those things will not build the discipline that helps me achieve my goals.

Delayed Gratification

When you take a stand as a leader and make important decisions, you won't always receive instant gratification. If you do, be on your guard, because it may not last long. In fact, things typically get more difficult after a hard decision is made. You may even feel all alone and wonder if you did the right thing.

Jim was willing to put off popularity and comfort for a larger cause. He wanted to start a Kindness Movement in his middle school, but this was in a school where being selfish and picking on others was very common. At first he was laughed at; many mocked him in the halls. But the more they laughed, the nicer he became. He was even nice to the very people who made his life so miserable. Eventually, his conviction and enthusiasm proved contagious.

His conviction and enthusiasm were contagious.

All of the stories in this book come from real situations, but know that the names have been changed to protect each person.

15

Q: Describe how you could put in more time to be better prepared to do your very best in the following areas: (write out answers for each)

Studying:

Practicing for your sport:

Focusing more on your friend(s) than yourself:

Thinking ahead of time before you follow someone and do something wrong:

Showing your family how much you appreciate them:

Q: What does delayed gratification mean to you?

Q: Why do you think it is so hard for so many of us to spend the time alone -- preparing and studying and putting in the time to insure we do things at our best -- instead of merely doing what is easy and comes natural?

Q: Tell of a time when you put forth real effort into something important and you performed at your best:

Q: How did you feel about yourself because of your hard work and accomplishment?

Q: Now, describe a situation where you were lazy and didn't prepare as you could have, and performed at a level too low for your ability:

Q: Can you see that you let yourself and others down because you did what was easy and didn't live out delayed gratification?

People admired Jim's determination and loving attitude toward those who tried to ruin his dream. By the end of the semester, Jim and some others made a big banner in the school's entrance. It was called the Kindness Board. Whenever someone received a kind act from another student, they wrote it on the board and signed it. They wrote things like: "Yesterday Larry Smith stood up for me during football practice and I sure appreciate it." This particular entry was signed by Bob. On another entry a girl wrote, "I want the entire school to know that I saw Julie Andrews sit by a new student on Tuesday. It impressed me and I think we all should be more like her."

Because Jim took a risk and stuck by his decision even when it was difficult, he was finally able to see the rewards of his work; and everyone entering the school could read the inspiring testimonials of students who admired each act of kindness. It inspired others to notice kind acts; more importantly, it inspired others to perform acts of kindness themselves.

Hardship

Hardship will not deter a true leader. When things get tough for others, leaders keep on going.

Have you ever thought about what it takes for single parents to keep food on the table and all of the bills paid, and still raise their kids with both love and discipline? They often have a hard time with their thickheaded children, but they never give up. Neither can you, if you want to be a leader. Will you hang in there when:

- People don't praise you for doing something difficult?
- You do the right thing, and aren't even noticed?
- The newspapers never print your news?
- No one lights up Broadway with your name?
- People get angry at you for taking a stand?

Worth the Cost

As you have seen above, if you decide to lead others, you will pay a price in terms of sacrifice, time, delayed gratification, and hardship. As a result, some days you'll struggle to find your way or get the energy you need.

"What's the use then?" you may ask. "I could never be that perfect. I may as well give up today."

Do you think that to be a leader, you must:

- Never get tired?
- Never feel unimportant?
- Never differ from the crowd?

If so, you've either set your expectations too high or misunderstood my message. Everyone poops out, makes mistakes, and has regrets. That's why it's so important for you to realize that you can't become the kind of person I'm talking about on your own. To succeed, you'll need to stay in close touch with your family and true friends, as well as teachers and mentors who believe in you. It's vital that you stay strong by getting the needed encouragement that we all need at times to carry on – encouragement from people who know your frailties and can help you overcome them. Find people who will challenge you to be someone special.

Q: What hardships have you overcome?

Q: Tell of someone you admire who has lived through a hard situation and not complained about it:

Q: Tell of some things you could do to make the best of a tough situation without complaining:

4 Leadership Do's

"Setting an example is not the main means of influencing others, it is the only means."
– Albert Einstein

You'll have to do three things to become a leader:

1. Start right where you are.

How well you are known by others won't necessarily be a reflection of your leadership skills, but who you are and what you do will have a lot of impact on whether or not you become a leader. So don't wait to become famous or popular before you start to lead.

Frequently (but not always), people who lead well become known for the quality of their lives. Even when the papers never pick up on the stories of people who feed the homeless or seek to bring reconciliation to warring parties, for example, their touch on the lives of people around them can have a powerful impact.

Remember, leadership starts with you and your own willingness to become the kind of person others can admire and respect. You do that by filling your life with good character qualities and wise decisions. These qualities lie within you. Your job is to bring them out in the open.

2. Have something worthy to believe in, and be willing to stand up for it.

Leaders have a goal worth reaching for -- one that may not include popularity, gaining everyone's agreement, or getting elected class president. What are you willing to take heat about and not give up? Identify those things that are worth the pain. What cause or purpose can you get that excited about?

People who lead -- really lead -- put themselves out for others, even when it's uncomfortable.

3. Pay the price.

Leading others means you have to pay a price. For example, you may lose friends and have to give up watching your favorite TV show because you've given time in your schedule to helping someone with a problem. Perhaps you'll stand out because you suffer for what you believe in. Still, the real way to leadership is fighting for what you know is right, following your heart, living out the dreams that are inside you, and settling for nothing less.

Q: What misconceptions have you had about leadership? List them below. Do you have a hard time giving them up?

Q: How did you develop your ideas of leadership? Name a few things that have influenced how you think about being a leader:

Q: What people have you looked up to as leaders? Name three people you admire from history, today's world scene, or your personal life. Why do you admire those people? Do they fit the definition of leadership that we've considered here?

Q: How do you stack up against these leadership qualities?

5 How Do I Build a Good Reputation?

"People will forget what you said, They will forget what you did, But they will never forget how you made them feel."

– Maya Angelou

Much of your reputation will come from the things you do. When you are active in your church group, school clubs, or community efforts, people will get to know you. If they see that you achieve, and that you make wise decisions, they'll tend to think well of you. If you do things that don't earn respect, you'll earn a reputation for doing the wrong thing (for choosing unwisely), and most people will not think highly of you.

Sadly, lots of people may even scoff at the idea that you need a good reputation.

When Rick encouraged Sally to have sex with him and she turned him down, he asked, "You don't care what other people think, do you?"

Sally thought a moment. She didn't want him to get the idea that she was easily influenced by others, but the fact was that she did care about her reputation. "Yes," she answered. "I guess I do care what others think. I have a strong set of values and beliefs that my family and I believe in, and I don't want to do anything that would make our family name look bad. When people know what I believe, and see me doing something wrong, they will look at me as a hypocrite."

That situation made Sally think about why she dated Rick. If he thought having sex was okay, they didn't share an understanding of what was right and wrong. In a little while, she decided she didn't want to date Rick if it meant risking having sex with him.

25

Sally made a wise decision. She had been taught that a good name is better than fitting in for the moment. Though she missed Rick for a while, in the end she knew she could not have lived with herself if she had given in to his demands. As she spent time with her real friends at school, she felt encouraged that, though she had given up a few dates, she had maintained her self-respect and the respect of others. "I don't have to date to like myself. If it's a choice between feeling good about myself and going out on a Friday night, I'll do the thing that builds my self-esteem," she shared with a friend.

For Fred, it wasn't a matter of dating, but of doing well in school. Though his teachers said he could get high grades, he never seemed to. There was always a game to go to, a friend who needed help, or a job to do at home. Homework always seemed at the bottom of his list of priorities.

Finally, a counselor pointed out to Fred that his chances for getting into college were slipping away. "Sure you can go out and work once you finish high school, but is that the kind of future you want for yourself? Getting a job at McDonald's seems fine now, but you can't support a family on what you'd make there, and you won't have many skills to offer an employer. You'll make more money once you have an education, and you have the brains to do it. I hate to see you waste your chances because you don't want to do homework."

Fred thought about that, and started making some changes. He still keeps in touch with his friends, but only after he's finished his homework. Now instead of spending one hour studying for a test, he spends a whole evening. The difference in his grades is startling, and so is the change in the opinion of his teachers.

"I knew you could do it," said his counselor. "You've got a lot to share with other people, as long as you do it the best way. I'd be happy to see you counseling people for a living -- you seem to do it naturally -- but don't let that get in the way of the goals you need to set today."

Changing Your Reputation

Do you need to develop a new reputation? Start today, using a simple four-step plan:

1. Discover what you have done wrong. Fred and Sally had been making some unwise choices that they needed to change. Before they could change, however, they had to identify the problem. Don't be like Fred and wait for someone to walk up and tell you. Take a look at your own life and head off the problems.

Q: Have people ever told you they think you're making a mistake?

Q: Have they tried to steer you away from a decision?

Q: Think through their advice, and evaluate where you are today. Were they right?

Q: Do you find yourself in a place you hate because you made a bad choice?

Q: Go back, look at your mistake. What you need to do to correct it.

Write out your thoughts and answers to these questions. Remember, the answers will help you learn about yourself, and learning about yourself is an important step in the process of becoming the best possible person you can be. Be honest, and spend the time (delayed gratification) to answer them correctly. What you put into this exercise is what you will receive out of it.

27

2. Make amends, if necessary. Lyle had lied to his father about the places he went on Saturdays. Now they didn't talk about where he went on the weekends, but Lyle's relationship with his father was hurting.

After he attended a leadership course offered at his school, Lyle knew he had to apologize to his dad.

"Dad," he said, "I know I've been wrong in the places I've gone and the things I've done on the weekend. I'm sorry for that -- and I'm even sorrier that I lied to you about it. Can you forgive me?"

Lyle's father forgave him, but it took a while to reestablish trust between them. Every weekend Lyle made sure his dad knew what was going on. He even spent some time at home. When his dad saw that Lyle was where he said he'd be, he knew his son had changed. Now they have a better life together.

Only by admitting you were wrong and taking responsibility for your mistake can you bring healing to a broken relationship. You may have to give the other person time, just as Lyle didn't see the full measure of his dad's forgiveness for a while; but with patience and faithfulness, you too may have a better relationship. If things don't work out, at least you will have the peace that comes with knowing you have done your best. Leave guilt behind and move on with your life.

Q: Do you need to apologize, give back something you've stolen, or make up to someone for a mistake?

28

3. Develop a new plan. Once you know what you've done wrong, and have identified your mistakes, make a plan that will keep you from repeating the mistakes. For Sally, that meant deciding not to date someone who did not share her thoughts on saving yourself for your future spouse. "I thought Rick believed as I do, but I was wrong. What happened between us convinced me I need to choose my dates more carefully. Now I get to know someone much better before I go out with him. If he does not share my values and beliefs, I feel free to turn him down." She may not date as much as before, but Sally is happier in her new plan. "When a boy treats you well, you have a much better dating relationship. Now that I'm seeing David, I know what was wrong between Rick and me."

Q: What area in your life do you need to develop a plan so you don't do the same foolish thing that has gotten you into trouble in the past?

Q: Who could you go to for advice on how to better handle this situation if and when it comes up again?

---

4. Put your plan into action. When Lyle decided to be honest with his parents, he made it a practice to call them when he changed his plans. It was a pain at times to have to stop and call, but it sure helped his parents trust him. If they needed to call him, they knew where he was; and on the occasions when they did call, he proved he was trustworthy. Eventually, the cost of a few phone calls paid a great bonus. The new relationship with his parents is something Lyle never thought could happen. "I couldn't give enough money to have this kind of family life," Lyle shared. "A short time of trouble is worth it."

What plan are you going to put into action starting today?

Write down 3 steps that you are going to do to make sure your plan gets accomplished:

Improving Your Reputation

Perhaps you don't have a problem with stealing, lying, or cheating. Still, you don't need to have a "big" problem to get a reputation you'd like to change.

"I had a reputation for being a real snob," Beth shared. "People thought I didn't think much of them, but the real person I doubted was myself. 'Will people like me?', I kept wondering, and I wanted them to. I just felt afraid to open up to them.

"Finally I took a look at what my life's really like.

"When I make friends, I keep them for a long time. People like me when they get to know me, but I make it hard for them to do that. Saying hello or adding to someone's conversation takes courage for me, but I try to do it anyway. Now I know I do have something to offer and that people want to know me, and I'm reaching out in spite of my doubts. You know, there are a lot of nice people out there -- and I used to turn them off!"

Is your own attitude getting in your way? Take a look at the way you think about yourself and others, and how you treat people. Which of these describe you? Circle the numbers below that you best identify with.

People Quiz

1. I like people, and treat them as if they are important.

2. I am afraid of others and what they might do to me or say about me.

3. When others share their feelings, I listen carefully and give them good feedback.

4. When a friend has a problem and comes to me, he wants answers. I jump right in with all the advice I can give.

5. If someone compliments me for a good job, I say, "Thank you," politely.

6. When someone says I've done well, I respond, "Oh, anyone could do that."

7. If a friend is quiet, I try to invite her into my conversation.

8. I always have good ideas, so when I talk, I tell others about them. If anyone else wants to say something, it's too bad.

9. I learn from other people, so I like to listen to their ideas.

10. Other people always have better ideas than mine. If my ideas are any good, someone else will eventually come up with them.

11. People who are different from me are interesting. I like to discover what they are like.

12. People who aren't my friends aren't my type. If I don't spend time with them, it won't matter.

13. My family is important to me. Even if they aren't perfect, I want my family to be as good as possible. I'll spend time to make it that way.

14. My family doesn't matter at all, but my friends do. I won't be at home if I can go out with my buddies instead.

Make an effort to develop the attitudes expressed in the odd numbered answers on the above quiz. Do you:

- Listen carefully to others?

- Encourage people when they feel down?

- Share your own problems with friends?

- Try not to complain about every little trouble?

- Accept people who don't agree with you, look like you, or have your background?

- Do what you can to develop a strong family life?

- Appreciate people when they are kind to you or try to help you?

- Understand that no one is perfect?

If you focus on others, treat them with respect, and encourage them, you will build their respect. If you complain and tear them down, you will build a reputation for being difficult.

How do people see you? Are you seen as easy to talk to, kind, gentle, and considerate, or complaining, angry, and belligerent? Which would you rather be? Now is the time to take stock of yourself and develop the leadership and communication skills that can help you for a lifetime. Maybe you need to learn to listen more caringly, share your own problems with someone who can help, or improve your own opinion of yourself.

Remember, you can change and become the person you truly deserve to be. Everybody matters, and that means YOU. If it seems as if you have a lot of work to do, start now. You don't need to stay the same; a better reputation is waiting for you. It starts with you. It can start today. You are proving that you have what it takes by reading this book. If you haven't filled in the questions, please go back and do it before reading on. This book isn't about how fast you can get through it; rather, it's about you searching for and finding the real you. Only then can you do what you must to make the changes needed to be the kind of person you and others can admire.

6

My Self-Esteem
(How Good Is It?)

Self-Esteem test: What do you see in the following letters? (there are 2 answers)

IAMNOWHERE

I won't tell you I had the greatest image of myself as a teen. As you'll see later, I couldn't give the jocks any competition, and I didn't win any prizes when it came to grades. Being tall and skinny didn't help, either. Everyone kidded me about it at school.

In the eleventh grade I got a chance to start all over. When my dad got a job in another town, I moved from a Class-D high school in a small town to a Class-A high school. I never knew they built schools so big. My old school had maybe twenty doors in the whole place (including the restrooms). Now I had to contend with two floors, six wings, homerooms, and one million lockers! (At least it seemed like one million lockers.)

You might not believe this, but it took me three weeks to find my locker. I caught the bus in the morning and went to school. With barely enough time to go to all my classes and catch the bus at night, how could I look for my locker? So I kept my books in with a friend's. After I moved, I felt so shy that he was the only person I got to know.

Can you imagine that? I make a living talking about self-confidence and believing in yourself, but as a teen I couldn't even find my own locker. It probably doesn't take much to figure that something happened to change my opinion of myself. In this book I hope to share some of the ideas I later came in touch with, so that you won't have to wait three weeks to find your locker if you move.

Let's Take a Look at Self-esteem

Before we examine your self-esteem, let me point out several very important things.

1. No one has perfect self-esteem. By this, I mean that no one feels totally happy with himself all the time. Everyone has ups and downs. Having bad days is perfectly normal. If I never had my low times, I wouldn't appreciate the good ones, and I wouldn't have anything to strive for.

2. Self-esteem (how you feel about yourself) responds to exercise like a muscle. It might seem shabby now, but with effort and practice, it can grow as strong as anyone's. That's right! No matter how low you feel about yourself today, you can apply certain principles and practice certain techniques to raise your self-esteem to a happy, healthy level. Start getting excited now about the positive you of the future!

3. We'll take inventory on how you see yourself (The self-esteem quotient quiz will come up soon.). Realize this: Everyone has negative parts in his/her self-esteem. Once you've identified yours, you can work on these areas if you choose. Notice, I said if you choose. It remains entirely up to you what you do about the actions and beliefs in your life that drag you down and keep you from feeling great about yourself. No one can, or will, do it for you. I must say, I feel proud of you for sticking with this book so far. You started on your way. Don't stop now!

In the following test, you'll notice that there are two sets of thirty statemnts: one set contains negative statements, and the other contains positive statments. For each number, compare the statements between the two columns, and place a check beside the sentence or situation that best fits you. You'll have some answers in each column if you're honest. We will grade it when you finish.

Test Your SEQ (Self-Esteem Quotient)

Negative

If you have a low self-esteem (you don't believe in yourself):

1. I expect to fail most of the time.
2. I can't stand it if others laugh at me.
3. I don't have many friends, and I am very jealous!
4. I feel uneasy when I am alone.
5. My attitude is, "It doesn't matter what I do. I don't care anyway."
6. I hate criticism, and I get mad at the person who tries to help me.
7. I blame others.
8. It's almost impossible for me to forgive or forget that someone hurt or made fun of me.
9. I feel successful when I have lots of new clothes, a giant music collection, a new car, computer, and so on. (I love my material things.)
10. I think, "No one wants to go on a date with me."
11. I'm loud in class and during assemblies. I figure, "Why should others enjoy it and learn? I'm not going to."
12. I go along with the crowd most of the time.
13. I join in with others when they are putting someone down.
14. I only do what is expected of me, and no more, on my job.
15. I come late to my job and take long breaks. Besides, everyone else does.
16. I accept a date with just about anyone.
17. I smoke cigarettes.
18. I go to any movie, especially if it is a top hit.
19. Sex before marriage is okay if you love someone.
20. I don't like my height, weight, ears, teeth, family, race, or color of skin.
21. Others would like me if I were better at sports, better looking, smarter, richer, and so on.

22. I try to do most of the talking. That way people think I'm smart and outgoing.
23. I'd do anything to be popular.
24. I try to do most of the talking. That way people think I'm smart and outgoing.
25. I'd do anything to be popular.
26. I laugh at all offensive or mean jokes if they're funny.
27. The "beat" is all that matters in my music.
28. I love to talk about others, and to gossip.
29. I hate it when authority figures tell me what to do.
30. I never ask questions in class.
31. I never talk to my parents about my problems and concerns. They wouldn't understand, and I'd probably get in trouble.
32. My parents work full-time, and there is no one for me to talk to, so I often feel worthless and confused.

Positive

If you have a healthy self-esteem (you believe in yourself):

1. I expect to be successful most of the time (grades, relationships, and so on).
2. It doesn't bother me if people laugh. I figure it's their problem, not mine.
3. I have lots of friends, and I give my boyfriend or girlfriend the freedom he or she needs.
4. I enjoy being alone at times, because I am my best friend.
5. I have a good attitude toward people, my future, school, my family, church, and so on.
6. I appreciate someone pointing out areas in which I can grow or become more effective.
7. I take responsibility for my actions, grades, and life.
8. I forgive others easily, because I know I make the same mistakes.
9. Material items are not nearly as important to me as people. I never flaunt my material things, because I would not want to hurt those who are less fortunate.

10. I think, "She'll probably love to go out with me. I'll go ask her." (If she says no, I say to myself, "You're not as smart as I thought you were!")

11. My respect for other people allows me to be quiet when others are talking.

12. I like being with the right crowds, but I always decide for myself what is good enough for me to do.

13. I've developed the courage to stand up for the person getting picked on.

14. I'm not the world's greatest worker, but I do try my best. I also look for extra ways I can be a good employee.

15. I'm no worse than my word. If I say I will be there at 3:00, you can count on it!

16. I only go out with others who believe in themselves, have a good moral foundation, and respect me.

17. My life is too important to ruin it with tobacco. I don't like to smell like smoke, either.

18. I think more of my friends and myself than to be exposed to filthy language and scenes.

19. Sex is reserved for after marriage, period! One thing I'll never lose is my self-respect. If I don't respect me, no one else will either.

20. I accept who I am fully and completely. Some areas I can change (grades, teeth, weight, bad habits) but some I can't (height, race, color, ears, family, handicaps).

21. I realize the best way to make friends is to be a friend to others first.

22. I realize we have two ears and one mouth, so I try to listen more than I talk. Then others know I am truly interested in them and their thoughts.

23. I love being popular, but I will never compromise on my principles or beliefs. I know that if I don't stand for something, I will fall for anything.

24. If something or someone is offensive, I never laugh.

25. I'm smart enough to know that damaging words and thoughts going into my mind will do me no good. (What goes in as words comes out as actions.)

26. I believe a simple phrase: "I will speak evil of no person."

27. I respect authority, even though I don't always agree with people.

28. If I have a question, I always ask for the answer. If anyone makes fun of my "dumb" question, I figure it is his problem, not mine.

29. Even when I find it hard, I always try to talk to my parents about my concerns, problems, and fears. They have their problems as well, so quite often I have to make the first move.

30. Though my family and I are very busy, I always find time to open up and share with the special people in my life – like my parents (when it is a convenient time), my coach, and other close friends.

How Did You Do?

Now that you've had a chance to look at your reactions to your own self-image, let's see what causes the trouble spots. We'll take a look at the things that keep us from being our best.

25-30 positive = I like me a lot. You are doing really well. We'll work on the areas you need help on, and you will end up in great shape. Like an expensive race car, you need a little fine tuning.

18-25 positive = I'm okay, but nothing great. You look pretty good, but you can feel a lot better about yourself by working on your few negative areas. You have the capabilities of a Corvette if we get you some new tires (foundations) and put in some premium gas.

11-17 positive = I'm not exactly my best friend. You may feel like you have a long way to go, but you are closer than you think to having great self-esteem. Don't prepare yourself for the junkyard yet. While you do have some rust, we will contend with it in the upcoming pages.

0-11 positive = I think of myself as that weirdo in the mirror. You don't feel very happy with your life, and probably don't think you have much hope for improvement. I'm here to tell you there is a huge amount of hope. Together we will bring you to a point where you feel proud of what you believe in and who you are. Just follow the simple map on the next pages.

7

Self-Image Destroyers

"No one can make you feel inferior without your consent."
– Eleanor Roosevelt

Two elements cause us to think poorly of ourselves:

- The unfair comparisons we make when we measure ourselves against others
- The negative beliefs others have fed us and we have put faith in

Either one of these two elements can destroy your self-image, because each tells you that you are somehow not good enough. The good news is that you don't have to give in to such thought patterns. By becoming aware of how they work in your life, you can change how you think about yourself. Growing a good, healthy self-image will make you feel better about everything you do!

Unfair Comparisons

Unfair comparisons may come in lots of shapes and sizes, but they all make you miserable. When you measure yourself by someone else's yardstick, you'll never come up with an accurate view of yourself. Every time you look at someone else and try to become as "perfect" as he or she seems, you'll end up falling on your face, because you will have set unrealistic, impossible standards of perfection for yourself. Even so, most of us have tried to live up to someone else's idea of what's good in these areas:

- Talents
- Physical beauty
- Intelligence
- Actions

41

Unfair Comparisons:
When you measure
yourself by someone else's
yardstick, you'll never
come up with an accurate
view of yourself.

What someone else thinks is good for him isn't necessarily right for your life. Yet, before you know what's right for your own life, you'll need a clear view of yourself and your abilities. So let's see how this kind of thinking touches those four areas mentioned above.

Talents. Have you ever thought something like "I'm so weak and skinny, and he's the big man on the wrestling team," or, "I can't play the drums, and she's great at it"? When you do this, chances are you're concentrating on the other person's strong points and your weak ones -- so of course you come up looking bad! It's like throwing a pair of loaded dice: You can't win.

Instead, when you find yourself thinking this way, realize that everyone has some talents, but no one has all of them. Maybe the wrestler feels so shy that he can't talk to anyone without getting tongue-tied; or maybe the girl who plays the drums just flunked math. In the same way, you shouldn't expect yourself to be good in every area. Learn to just focus on the things you do well -- and enjoy them.

Remember:
Only compare yourself
against what you could
be doing or what you
could become. Don't
judge yourself by
someone else's gifts.

How have you compared yourself against others in your school?

What are you going to do from now on instead of comparing yourself against them?

Physical Beauty. Hollywood ... I'm sick of it! Not everyone looks like your favorite movie star or model, so don't let your face or body stop you from making the most of your life. Phyllis Diller didn't try to look like the cover girls. She took her talent (humor) and made it into success. Jimmy Durante took his giant nose (a lemon) and turned it into lemonade.

When it comes to physical-beauty problems, I can really understand. My experience with them goes back a long way. When I was in second grade, I saw a group of kids looking at me and giggling. Then the biggest one pointed his finger at me and said real loud, "Look at him. He's skinny." (He really had a way with words.) They saw my four most protruding features: my knobby knees and my bony elbows.

I went crying home from school, ran up to my dad, and said, "Da-Da-Dadd-Daddy [my bottom lip wouldn't stop quivering], they called me skinny." He looked down and said, "Well, you are skinny." He was trying to make me laugh, but it didn't work.

With that I went to my room and made a pact with myself that no one would ever again call me skinny (at least not because they saw my bony knees and elbows). I promised never to be seen in public in shorts or a short-sleeved shirt. Being a boy of my word – until I reached seventeen – I never wore such clothing. Can you imagine that? I was seventeen years old before I had the confidence to let my elbows and knees publicly see daylight!

All those years I wore pants cut off or rolled up to just below my knees, and shirts that covered my elbows. I figured that when others didn't see those parts of my anatomy, they'd think I had lots of muscles up there.

Today my story proves the importance of perception. I no longer call my physique skinny -- now it's "trim and fit"!

Look at yourself in a positive way.

Remember:
Don't see yourself
through Hollywood's
eyes.

List some positive things you are going to notice about yourself instead of looking at others?

Intelligence. You'll know you've fallen into the intelligence comparison trap when you think things like, "I'm not as smart as John in math, so I must not be as good a person," or "Mary got a scholarship to a good college, and I missed out, so I'm a flop." Making the most of your intelligence doesn't mean you have to be an Einstein, but you should do the most you can with the mental gifts you do have.

I never fooled anyone into thinking I was one of the smartest kids in my class. In fact, I ranked in the part of the class that made the upper 50 percent possible. I even had bad breath. But since then I've learned that bad breath is better than no breath, and the lower half of the class is better than no education at all.

Remember:
Each of us has special interests and abilities; this includes intellectual talents. Study hard in the areas you do well in, and others will see you as a highly intelligent person.

Write down some of your gifted areas:

How does it make you feel now that you have described some of the smart parts of you?

Actions. When you judge yourself against others' actions, it gets awfully hard to look good. Doing so may mean that because you couldn't get a part in the class play, you feel like a zero; or because the teacher didn't mention your speech as the best one she's heard all year (but she did mention your friend's), you're a moron; or because you got cut from the team, you're a klutz. It's important for you to remember: If you fail one popularity poll, don't see yourself as a loser.

One year I went out for the football team (a stupid thing for a skinny kid to do). Because I didn't want to get my uniform dirty, I felt afraid to block anyone.

In the first game of the year, I played defensive end; and it just so happened that the very first play of the game was an end-around run. That meant that everyone on the other team had one purpose in life for the next eight-and-a-half seconds: *to kill me!* My first glimpse of the immediate future came when I heard the offensive end -- the fellow staring me in the eye -- mention the word "kill". As I saw the members of the other team run at me, my mind began to work fast. It's short, sweet little talk went something like this: "Hey, turkey, you're gonna die!"

I responded the way any red-blooded, young, scared, wanting-to-be-popular-but-not-at-all-costs American kid would have: I hit the dirt! The guys on the other side ran right over me for the touchdown. That was my only play in organized football. The coach pulled me out of the game, and I quit the next week. Now, to further encourage my self-esteem, someone labeled me Skinny Chicken Sanders.

There was no way I could believe that I had played my role well -- and role-playing is what our actions are all about (I also learned something about a talent I didn't have.). If I had believed that was the best job I'd ever do at anything, my self-esteem would have been as flat as my body was after two tons of football players finished digging their cleats into me. But, I'm glad it didn't all end there.

When you use any of these judgments on yourself, you're setting impossible standards. If you think about it, you'll probably realize that there is not a person alive who never fails at anything. Sure, it might seem that way if you barely know a person, and only see him during his good times; but even the football-playing honor student, who has all the girls in the class dying to date him, has problems.

When I was in school, I wanted to be like the jocks. They seemed special. They had their own table in the cafeteria. They didn't eat like everyone else (they only used their bare hands). They didn't carry their books like the rest of the guys. These apes could take the biggest dictionary in the school

Remember:
Your identity should always rate a 9 or 10. Your role might deserve a 1 or - 3, but that can't change your importance as a person. Don't let poor performance lower your perception of yourself.

45

and hold it down at one side, arm straight. When they took their giant steps, they grunted like Tarzan's jungle buddies.

Just once, I wanted to be a jock and walk through the halls, hearing the girls sing "How Great Thou Art". Well, I never did, and I never will live up to my own impossible standard. You probably can't live up to some things you'd like to do, either. But you can live up to a higher goal than any you've probably ever thought about.

What's the solution to all these unfair-comparison problems? First of all, learn to treat yourself as the special unique person you truly are. Next, don't blame others for what bothers you, and be willing to take responsibility for your actions. If you can follow these steps, and apply the other principles of this book, you will be well on your way to feeling great about yourself.

Almost every time I go out to speak, I meet people who have a healthy self-esteem as a direct result of their belief that they were meant for something good in this life. I've never met a person who truly had a healthy self-esteem and peace of mind who didn't believe in something bigger than themselves. Unfortunately, while many people look or act successful on the outside, they can't stand themselves on the inside. The advice in this book will help you live with yourself and achieve the great things you were meant for.

Write down several things you have just learned about how damaging it can be to compare yourself against others:

Check Out Your Turf

1. If you haven't tested your self-esteem,
go back to the SEQ test and answer all the
questions. Now take a look at the answers.
What are your biggest strong points?
What are your biggest weak points?

2. Which of the weak points in your self-esteem
result from unfair comparisons?
Which ones result from negative beliefs
fed to you by others?
Who have you compared yourself to?
Has anyone ever told you that you didn't
measure up?

3. How have you made unfair comparisons
in your talents? ... physical beauty? ...
intelligence? ... actions? Why are such
standards impossible to achieve?
How can you start treating yourself as if
you're not a monkey?

4. What negative messages have you
believed in? Why are they wrong?
How can you start fighting back?

8 Negative Beliefs That Crush Self-Esteem

"I care not what others think of what I do, but I care very much about what I think of what I do. That is character."

– Theodore Roosevelt

Even when we don't compare ourselves to some ideal that we could never live up to, we still have bad opinions of ourselves based on the thinking of other people:

- The negative things the world says to us
- The negative messages of the media
- The negative words others say to us
- The negative messages we get when people don't say something to us
- The negative reactions of others to our situation

What the World Says. We don't live in an upbeat world. Society gives us an opinion of ourselves that isn't very complimentary in most cases. If you don't have the latest clothes or the most expensive music system, you'll probably feel like an outcast if you fall for this line. By trying to keep up with the constantly changing views of society, you'll drive yourself nuts!

When I tell you that seven out of ten people have negative attitudes, you'll begin to understand why our society acts so negative. We all seem to focus on the bad things in life more easily than we appreciate the good ones. At that rate, it doesn't take long for everything to look pretty bleak.

Media Messages. Every newscast tells about a tragedy. Books and magazines that describe the world today don't make it sound too promising. While not many of them will help you attack the world's negative thinking, some good, uplifting books, CDs, television programs, and so on do

Remember:

Look for the positive. It's out there; you, however, are the one that has to find it.

In what ways have you become negative like much of the world around you?

49

exist. If you just turn on the boob tube and watch anything or listen to any radio show – without deciding what's good for you – you'll reflect the same attitude the media have. Give yourself something better!

In what ways have you become negative like much of the world around you?

What can you do to turn this trend around?

Describe some of the daily doses of negative stinking thinking you have allowed to come in to your mind from the media:

What Others Say. Anything someone else tells you about yourself you may believe more than your own opinion of yourself -- especially if it's something negative. Even if that person is dead wrong, you seem to put faith in his words when he tells you you've been stupid, ugly, uncoordinated, or whatever. Somehow others always have more credibility to us than we do to ourselves.

Remember:
As a young adult, you can only blame yourself for not putting good, clean, positive thoughts into your mind.

Maybe that's why embarrassment seemed a permanent part of my younger years. I once thought a lot of what others might think, and I always seemed to live up to their worst expectations. One example was the time in the fourth grade when I made another graceful move as a maturing young man.

Do you know what can happen if you daydream with a pen your in mouth? Well, when I looked at the pen, all the ink was gone. I felt my lip; there was ink on my finger, which had now turned blue. I thought, "That's a weird place for ink." [I didn't really think; I just threw it in.] I did think, "No wonder you're so popular. You're always doing such cool things. I wonder if it's poisonous? I think I'm going to die!"

I passed a note to my friend Kenny. It read: "Can I trust you with something real personal? I don't want to be embarrassed." He read it and whispered back to me, "Sure you can. I'm your friend." I gave him a second note, which read, "I've got ink in my mouth. Find out if it's poisonous." He whispered back, "Don't worry, you can trust me. What are friends for anyway?" (Kenny was about to show me.) Then at the top of his lungs my pal shouted, "**Mrs. Smith, Bill's got ink in his mouth. Will he die?**"

Remember:
Some people find fault as though there were a reward for it.

I felt so embarrassed. I thought I would die as the class burst out laughing, and I ran to the bathroom to wash my own mouth out with soap. They didn't even need to use words to humiliate me: laughter spoke more clearly than any words my class could have spoken. What a fool!

You can try hard, but you'll never look perfect to everyone. If you don't make a mistake all on your own, occasionally someone will help you to make one. Plenty of people will gladly think bad thoughts about you, too (remember the seven out of ten). If you let it bother you, you'll just wear yourself out keeping track of them. Don't take it too seriously.

Briefly describe how you have been affected by the negative things others have said about you:

When People Don't Say Something. At times you may find yourself waiting for others to praise you or give you

51

accepting nods. If your friends or family or teachers don't notice you, you feel they don't care.

While you wait for such boosts to your ego, bring along plenty of camping equipment – you'll stay in the same place for a long time. So when the provisions run out and you decide to pull down the tent, try something that works better: take responsibility for becoming your own encourager and best friend. Give yourself rewards when you do something that makes you proud of yourself. Don't wait for the world to notice your accomplishments. If you don't develop habits of loving and comforting yourself, you'll grow up into a lonely adult.

That is worth repeating. Read these words very slowly and carefully. Take responsibility for becoming your own encourager and best friend. Give yourself rewards when you do something that makes you proud of yourself. Don't wait for the world to notice your accomplishments. If you don't develop habits of loving and comforting yourself, you'll grow up into a lonely adult.

Just because you don't have a lot of support and help, don't think you can't make it. If no one's pulling for you, listen to this story.

There once was a child who only wanted to become an actress. At eighteen she went from her home in upper New York State, to New York City, where she enrolled in a well-acclaimed acting school. After three months of hard work and total dedication, the school sent her mother a letter. It read, "Our school has produced some of the greatest actors and actresses the United States, and even the world, has ever known. However, we have never had a student with less talent and ability than your daughter. She is no longer enrolled in our school."

What a shock! A lifetime of dreams and wants could have been totally ruined by one letter, but not for this determined girl. Being kicked out of school and told she was worthless only made her more determined.

For the next two years she took all sorts of jobs to earn enough money to live on. She applied at almost every tryout that came along. She always heard the same thing, "You will never become an actress. You have no talent or ability!"

This aspiring actress came down with a severe case of pneumonia that so weakened her legs that the doctors told her she would never walk again. How do you react to such a terrible situation? Not only won't anyone support your desire to act, but now you can't walk. She worked with weights on each leg, and after two long and painful years of therapy, she could walk. She had a limp, but she worked hard to conceal it.

At age twenty-one she returned to New York City to try again. Guess what? She was turned down for eighteen years. That's right -- eighteen years! Only when she was forty years old did she finally got her first substantial acting job. Was it worth it? To her it was. In 1953, over 40 million people watched her television special. Her name? Lucille Ball. She wasn't born talented or great or beautiful. She had no breaks, and she didn't know important people, but she stuck to it. Stick to your dreams and desires, and you too can walk tall and proud.

Remember:
You need to be your own
coach and encourager.

Write out some of the ways you can be your own coach and push yourself towards your dreams:

Reactions of Others. If you have a problem with something in your life -- your family situation, past, color, or a physical handicap -- it gets easy to put the blame elsewhere: "My family is poor and uneducated, so I'll always be like them"; "I've been a loser all my life -- I can't change now"; "It's my race [or color] that holds me back"; "If I hadn't had that accident as a kid, it'd be different." The excuses are endless, but you don't have to give in to them.

When your situation seems unbearable, and you feel you can't go a step farther, think about people you know or have heard of who are making the most with what they

53

have. In the movie "Remember the Titans", one of the best football players on the team was paralyzed as a result of a car accident. Instead of feeling sorry for himself and giving up, he set his sights on the Olympics for people in wheelchairs. He went on to compete in them and was a great success. The point is that there is a need for each of us to look forward and not let circumstances get the best of us.

If you find yourself down and hurting, help someone less fortunate, and watch your own situation improve.

Remember:
The history books are filled with great people from every walk of life, every color and creed, and every possible awful situation. Let their stories inspire you to do what it takes to become your best.

How have you blamed others for something in your life?

Describe how you can take responsibility for what happens to you:

Fighting Back

How many of the various image destroyers and negative beliefs have influenced you? Everyone has fallen into such traps at one time or another, and just because you know what a particular one feels like doesn't mean you necessarily have a major problem in that specific area. So, pick out only the ones you experience most often. Now that you're aware of them, make positive efforts to change your wrong thinking. The next chapter will show you how.

When you start to put some of these steps into action – like the teen who wrote me the following letter – you'll have a better opinion of yourself:

"I never thought it was possible to believe in myself. After I heard you speak and say how special and unique I was I started to believe it. Now everything I do is different. I believe in ME!"

9 Building A Positive Self-Image

"To be yourself in a world that is constantly trying to make you something else is the greatest accomplishment."

– Ralph Waldo Emerson

Now that we've looked at the need for self-improvement, let's see what we can do about building a self-image that really works. I'd like to share with you ten steps to becoming your own best friend.

Step 1: Don't Compare Yourself With Others.

Compare yourself with you. Do you realize that if you were the only person in the world, you might feel lonely, but you would probably have a healthy self-esteem? If you didn't look around at others in school and see kids who seemed better-looking, richer, happier, and more coordinated, you wouldn't see yourself in a negative light. Picture this: three sisters who are triplets. All three are the prettiest in the entire school. All the other girls envy their beauty, but all three are the unhappiest girls in their class. Why? It's because they compare themselves with each other. Each one thinks the other two look better, so they all feel miserable. What a shame!

If you compare yourself with others, try to engage in positive comparison. Learn to look at the positive qualities, characteristics, or learned skills that others possess, and then use them to challenge yourself. Only look at areas in your life that you can change. You can't compare looks; we can't do much to change our looks. You can't compare family background or height; we can't change those, either. But you can desire another's dedication to practice, his honesty and respect for others, or her developed memory (By the way, each of us has a great memory. It is either trained or untrained. So if you forget something, just say, "It's my memory – it's untrained.").So if you forget something just say, "It's my memory—it's untrained").

55

Even though we just spent all of the last chapter talking about the harm of comparing yourself against others, write down your plan for not doing it any more in your life:

Step 2: Become Really Good at Something.

Find your "thing", do it, and do it well. People who believe in themselves, and can hold their heads high and look others in the eye, almost always have their "specialty". They've become really good at something, and it doesn't matter what it is! Ask yourself, **"What am I good at? What skills seem to come naturally to me? What am I willing to work hard at and practice over and over? What would I like to excel in?"** Find your song and sing it. Please believe me when I say this: **Greatness lives in you!** I absolutely believe it. Say it to yourself over and over again: **"There is greatness in me. I will become really good at**

_____."

You see, the real winners of a marathon are those who give it their best -- their all. A friend of mine came in 124th out of over 300 runners in a marathon. That means 123 people came in before him. Yet, he still felt like a winner. He stood at the finish line and congratulated the rest of the runners who came after him. He said, "I compete against me, no one else. I ran my race today, and I'm proud that I finished and did my best."

My nephew, Andy, wasn't muscular and athletic like his cousins, with whom he was very close. For the first years of his life this bothered him, and he really didn't think much of himself. When he entered high school, he became interested in two hobbies. By practicing and spending many hours on these activities, he became the best he could. Today he plays the trumpet better than anyone else in his entire school. He is also an accomplished bird watcher. He has made positive identification of more birds in his state of Ohio than 95 percent of the people his age. Andy now has self-esteem. He believes in himself. He didn't worry about what he couldn't do, but instead went ahead and became really good at two things that lie within his interests. You can find your areas also.

Make a list of five things that you would like to become good at, and are willing to put the time and effort forth:

1. _____
2. _____
3. _____
4. _____
5. _____

Step 3: Develop a Well-Rounded Life.

Life is made up of 6 main areas: family; spiritual; mental; social; physical; and financial.

Do you spend most of your time in the social area of your life? Do you totally neglect your family? It is very important that you look over where you spend most of your time (because that is where your love and interests usually lie), and see if you are being fair to yourself and the other important people in your life.

In what areas could you be more rounded?

_____
_____

Step 4: Learn How to Be Motivated From Within.

What you tell yourself about yourself has a lot to do with how well-motivated you'll feel. Without even realizing it, you often give yourself messages about how you're doing -- whether you're a winner or a loser. Psychologists call this unconscious conversation with yourself "self-talk".

You can control the thoughts you feed yourself -- what you think about is up to you. Instead of focusing on the negative, turn to the positive.

Negative Self-talk

- I can't do it.
- I knew I'd flunk that test
- I'll never get picked for the lead part in the play.
- That's just my luck. Things never go right for me.
- Why is everyone looking at me? I bet my pants are unzipped.

Positive Self-talk

- I can do it. I know I can.
- That test score wasn't like me. I'm a winner. I'll do better next time.
- I can see it now: Opening night I'm the lead part, and it goes great
- I didn't do as well as I can, but I'll do better next time.
- People always look at me. It must be my new haircut. I knew they would like it.
- Don't listen to the negative voices of the world around you.

If The World Says

(A student in the hall) "Another lousy Monday." You say, "Monday is just a day. It is not lousy or good. We make it good. I think I will have a super, fantastic, good day today."

(The weatherperson) There is a sixty percent chance of rain today." You say, "There is a forty percent chance of sunshine today."

(Your friend) "If I don't get asked out for that date, I'll just die." You say, "I think I know your problem. You've been saying that for so long, he thinks you're dead!

"Look at that stop light." You say, "It's a 'go light'."

"I love the weekend." You say, "Not me -- I love the 'strong end'."

(A kid in the cafeteria) "I don't want the 'end' of that bread." You say, "Every loaf of bread I see has two 'beginnings'."

(Your brother) "I've got a 'cold'." You say, "I don't believe in colds. I did catch a slight 'warm' last winter."

(A teacher) "This is the toughest test you'll have all year." You say, "I like challenges. I will study extra hard and make it easy."

(A smart aleck at school) "I'm going to make more money than you this summer." You say, "Not unless you get a job in a mint. That's the only place people 'make' money. The rest of us earn it."

"Where do you live?" You say, "The corner of walk and don't walk."

"Is it a long walk?" You say, "If the light gets stuck."

"How far is it from your house to my house?" You say, "The same distance it is from my house to your house."

This week try noticing how most people respond with negative actions, words, and expectations. But don't let yourself get caught up with the rest of these negatrons. Go ahead and feel sorry for them, but don't follow their example.

Most of all, don't let yourself be caught up in such senseless negative attitudes and actions as I did in my junior year of high school.

One day as I walked down the hall in school, minding my own business, the unexpected happened: a Mack truck hit me. I fell to the ground with the laughter of my classmates ringing in my ears. Ok, it wasn't really a Mack truck; it was another student. Because he had been running behind me, I had no clue of what was happening until his large hand hit me with great force. Extending his arm and putting his full weight behind the shove, he had toppled me over effortlessly.

Remember:
Words are motivators moving us toward success or failure. If you let other people's negativisms affect you, you'll fall back into failure.

59

Picking myself up, I felt embarrassed and angry, yet I didn't have enough nerve to fight back. That didn't mean I forgot him, though; for the next two years I made it my goal to get even with him. Preferably, this would happen in front of the entire student body -- on video for the entire world to see.

In preparation, I began to get in shape. I ordered a muscleman outfit with giant horse pills, a book on becoming another Atlas, and two dumbbells. Guess who was really the dumbbell? I also enrolled in a karate class and worked for almost a year-and-a-half to attain new heights of glory. No one ever knew about my secret goal of beating this student up in front of everyone, but it kept burning inside me just the same.

I still can't believe that I spent a year-and-a-half of my life with one consuming aim: to get even. It was probably the biggest waste of time, and the most senseless ambition I've ever had. Getting even puts you on the same wavelength and level as the person you feel angry at. It also shows that you cannot control your own emotions. In my case, I had let someone else totally control me -- both what I thought about, and how I acted. He had forgotten the incident five minutes later, but with me it lasted a year-and-a-half. How stupid.

List some of the ways you see yourself talking negative in stead of positive:

Write down the positive thing to say instead of what comes naturally:

Step 5: Look Your Best at All Times.

People who are "dressed up", feel up. You don't have to have the most expensive clothes. Just be clean and neat. Your attitude changes when people say, "You look nice," or, "I like that shirt."

When could you dress up to feel better about yourself?

Step 6: Read Good Books and Listen to Motivating CD's.

Good biographies and autobiographies can help you learn from others' successes. Read about famous leaders in all areas of life, especially those who had well-rounded lives. Notice how some famous people never did well in one area. By studying others, you can see where you want to be strong and not make the same mistakes. Listen to CDs that will motivate you and help you believe in yourself and set new goals. Listen to teachers and speakers with positive, uplifting messages. Even boring speakers have good points if you will listen for them and pick them out.

After my junior year in college I read my first book, cover to cover. That's right. All through school I never read an entire book. I associated reading books with bookworms, and I didn't want to be a bookworm. One day I picked up a book by Dale Carnegie called: *How to Win Friends and Influence People*, and for the first time in my life I began to hear the same type of things that I am sharing with you now: that life is a cause and effect situation. What we do causes an effect. What we give out comes back. I read that if you smile, most people will smile back. I learned that if you plant corn, you can't get beans. If you plant good thoughts in your mind, bad actions for the most part will not come out. In the same way, when you plant bad thoughts over and over, good actions will not come out.

I got so excited after reading this book that I called the local Dale Carnegie people, and a salesman came and signed me up for the next course. Though it cost several hundred dollars, and I didn't know anything about it, I felt very excited.

In this fourteen-week public-speaking class, they get people on their feet to give short talks in front of the other classmates with the purpose of helping build self-confidence. During the fifth session, I received the best-speech award of the night. I even received a standing ovation. Two days later I received a card from Don Davies, the man who signed me up. It said, "In all my years with Dale Carnegie, I have never seen a standing ovation at anything other than a graduation ceremony. You have some kind of speaking talent in you. Keep it up. You will go a long ways."

The next week I actually felt afraid to go back, because now I had an image of being a good speaker to live up to. So I quit the class. That's right -- I quit! I didn't have a fear of failure. Like many people, I had a fear of success. "How can I outdo what I did before?", I asked myself. "If I do well, they will expect more from me. If I try my best now, they will think I can always do it."

Do you know what? Mr. Davies kept calling me for almost a year, and convinced me to go back and take the course again. He kept telling me I had a speaking talent. Even though I didn't believe him, I started the course a year later, just to get him off my back. This time I showed him that he had someone to believe in. I proved to him that all his effort had a purpose and a reason, because this time I didn't quit the course until the seventh session. That's right. After the seventh session I felt so afraid to get up there and speak that I quit again. The days I had a class I became nervous. I couldn't eat all day, because I was so afraid of that one minute speech. But do you know what he had the nerve to do? He called me up the very next day and said, "You're going to take it again. You are going to finish this thing."

Well, about three weeks later, in a neighboring town, because of Mr. Davies' persistence and belief in me, I took the class. I finished the course this time. I even ended up being an assistant in several other classes; and I sold the Dale Carnegie course for two years. It turned into one of the greatest, self-confidence builders in my life.

A year or so later, I got a hold of some motivational cassette tapes. The first one was called The Strangest

Secret, by Earl Nightingale. He simply states that the strangest thing in the world is that we become what we think about. Similarly, Solomon says, "As a man thinks in his heart, he becomes." If I think about success, I will become successful. If I think about failure, I will become a failure. If I think I will get good grades and picture in my mind getting good grades, most likely I will work hard and fulfill that vision.

I shared these cassettes with some friends, and before I knew it, several people were getting together on a regular basis to hear them. One day a friend of mine named Bill had an idea. He said, "Wouldn't it be something if we could have fifty or sixty people get together and listen to these and all grow and become more positive and successful?" We rented a large hockey stadium and hired seven other speakers. The greatest salesman in the world, Joe Girard, spoke. One of the most exciting female speakers ever to grace the platform, Marilyn Van Derbur, was there. The other speakers included Robert Schuller from the Crystal Cathedral, Wayne Dyer, who wrote Your Erroneous Zones, Earl Nightingale himself, Art Fettig (called Mr. Lucky), Dr. Denis Waitley, The Psychology of Winning expert, my friend Bill, and myself.

Bill acted as MC that day, and I spoke on the platform with everyone else. I felt scared to death. Of course, the real amazing thing was the fact that we sold over 6,000 tickets in our little town for this marvelous event. We found out a month later that a large rally like this had never been attempted in a town with a population smaller than 1 million people. Our town only has 100,000 in it, but you see what happened: we became what we thought about. We pictured success, and we went after it, and we just happened to get it.

We were like the bumblebee. It does not know that it cannot fly -- it just flies. Do you know that scientists have it proven that, based on our current understanding of science and aerodynamics, it should be impossible for the bumblebee to fly? Guess why it can do it? It doesn't bother reading their books; it just flies.

About halfway through the promotion of that rally, we met a man named Dale Maloney. He showed us that we could do it, because he had done it before. He showed us creative ways of selling tickets – knocking on doors and talking to people and using enthusiasm. He got my younger brother, Dale, so excited that he went for a Guinness world record. He wanted to make the most telephone calls in a one-month period. Even though he didn't get the record, he personally sold over 2,000 tickets.

My talk that day was entitled, "Find Your Song and Sing It". I wanted everyone to know that life was meant to be lived. There is a song in each one of us that needs to be sung. We need to shout it from the highest treetops.

Since that time, I have had the opportunity and blessing of sharing the platform with such notable speakers as Paul Harvey, Art Linkletter, Zig Ziglar, Dr. Norman Vincent Peale, President Ford, and President Reagan. Many thousands of young people all across the country have delighted me as I have shared the message that meant so much to me. I have since written 13 books, spoken to more than a million high school students, and personally answered over 10,000 teen letters and emails.

It all started when I read one book and listened to one cassette.

Make a plan right now for putting good, uplifting stuff in your brain:

Step 7: Try Something New Each Week!

Each week step out of your "comfort zone." Once you get into the habit of trying new things, your confidence level will grow by leaps and bounds.

Try one of these each week:

1. Introduce yourself to someone new.
2. Write someone a thank-you or an I-was-just-thinking-of-you note.
3. Ask at least one question per class. (Make sure it's a question that is on your mind. Don't just ask a nonsense question because I've suggested it.)
4. If the opportunity arises, give an oral book report instead of a written one.
5. Always look for opportunities to give a report, help take attendance, give a short speech, and so on. The greatest single confidence-building activity I know of is public speaking. You won't be perfect, but you will be one of the top 5 percent in your class when you give it a try! Others will admire your courage. Don't say you feel nervous, and no one will know.
6. Stop to help another student. For example, help someone who has just dropped his books, can't get his locker opened, needs help carrying something, or just needs some one to talk to.
7. Sit next to different people in the cafeteria. If you do this, others will start to notice you have more courage than they do. This will give you courage to keep growing.
8. Ask the teacher for extra work to do in area you enjoy. (By the way, this is not apple polishing. You are developing the attitude of doing more than expected. When you get in the job market, you will earn more than expected also.)
9. Look for a frown on another student's face, and be her friend. (Find a frown and turn it upside down.)
10. Help a lower-class person, or just be nice to him. Remember, what you give away to others comes back to you also.
11. Tell your mom and dad you love them and need to have some time alone with them to talk.
12. This one may give you heart failure, but try anyway. Be nice to your younger brother or sister. Specifically, ask if you can help on a project or with homework. (I told you it may cause serious health problems.)

13. Organize a homework night for three or four students who don't know the material as well as you do. This will be good leadership practice for you.
14. If you're old enough to take on a job, write a letter to a local business asking to have an interview concerning summer employment.

The summer I was seventeen, I tried something new: My friend Steve and I painted our way to California and back. By this, I mean we did the yellow lines on parking lots the whole way. We set a goal of $200.00 a day -- or we wouldn't sleep. We would knock on doors, ask for the job, and then we would open the trunk, get out the materials, and paint the lines on the parking lot.

For the next three summers I painted parking lots. It helped pay for a lot of my college education. Most of all, it gave me an identity. I came back to school with a new car. People didn't notice my car so much, but they did notice me walking taller. For the first time in my life I could do something that other kids couldn't do. I learned how to earn money. That is why I encourage you to find something that you can do and do well. Discover your burning desire inside.

Now make a list of your own. The important thing is not how well you do in these activities, but that you give them a try. You probably will find some unexpected things you really do well at. Go ahead; no one will develop your self-confidence for you. Winners and positive people pay the price by doing the things most others hate to do. Make that list.

Is it frightening for you to think of doing something new and different?

Who could you talk to about this that seems to be good at trying new things?

What are you going to do this week to step out of your comfort zone?

Step 8: Save Money!

Save at least 10 percent of every dollar you earn-preferably 20 percent. Living at home, you can do it. A friend of mine saved several thousand dollars from his paper route, in about five years. After high school he bought a house with his money. He had a better self-image just knowing he was able to save money while all his friends "blew" the money they had. I know, I always spent my money on the first thing that came along.

Do you have a way of making money?

When are you going to start saving?

Step 9: Make a Thankful List and a Success List.

A thankful list describes the abilities and talents and things you have been given without hard work and effort. A success list shows achievements you have accomplished because of hard work and effort.

Step A: Take a three-by-five card.
Step B: Put twenty things in each column.
               For example:

My Thankful List

A great family
A loving dad
A dedicated mom
My church
My eyesight
My legs
My ability to hear
My heart
My overall health
Living in America
Freedom of choice
My school
My many freedoms
Wise authorities in my life
My sports ability
My good looks
My singing talent
Sense of humor
Love for people
People's love for me

My Success List

I learned to talk
I learned to walk
I can tie my shoes
Hop
Ride a bike
Read
Read Treasure Island

Boy/Girl Scouts (all accomplishments)
Learned to drive
Built a model airplane
Baked a cake
Ate the cake [just kidding]
Good friendship with Mary
Quit complaining about getting up early
Stopped smoking
Lost five pounds
Got an A in English
Said no to drugs
Came home on time all last year [okay, one month]
My savings account

In short, this one little activity will help you become more confident, raise your self-esteem, believe in yourself, say no to peer pressure, rise above the crowd, become your best, and try harder to be better. Go to it! I know you can.

Write down 20 things you are thankful for (Remember, these are things you did not earn or work for; they were simply given to you.):

Now write out 20 things that you put effort towards and worked for:

Step 10: Smile, Look People in the Eyes, Be a Great Listener and Learn to Say Thank You!

These four simple yet seldom used activities will automatically put you on the trail toward a healthier self-esteem and more confidence.

By looking people in the eyes, you will feel better about yourself – and tuned into them as well. It's easier to trust those who have the confidence to look you in the eye. Plus, only when you have nothing to hide do you usually look others in the eye.

By becoming a great listener, you will be the person people like to be around. More people equals more friends, and more friends equals being able to influence more lives, thus making a larger contribution to the world we live in.

When you smile, you look happy. Others think you're happy, so they act happy around you. This chain reaction gives you even more reasons to smile.

By being a person who says, "Thank you," you will be one of the few people around who are developing the character quality of being grateful and thankful. Do you know that it has been said that it is almost impossible to be both grateful and depressed at the same time? I know from personal experience that when I am not thankful and am feeling sorry for myself, it is much easier to become depressed and have a feeling of hopelessness.

These 10 steps are like hidden gems of wisdom that many people either overlook, or they think they are too simplistic to actually try or live out on a regular basis. If you will give them a try and do your best to incorporate them into your life – maybe one each week – you will be living out the theme of this book. Every decision counts and everyone matters. Keep it up. You are well on your way to becoming the person you were meant to be, living out your potential instead of hiding it under a rock. I am very proud of you for all of the effort it takes to read this book and apply the principles in it. You should be proud of yourself as well.

10 Am I What I Do?

"One of the greatest things you have in life is that no one has the authority to tell you what you want to be. You're the one who'll decide what you want to be. Respect yourself and respect the integrity of others as well. The greatest thing you have is your self-image, a positive opinion of yourself. You must never let anyone take it from you."
– Jaime Escalante, teacher

You have been created in such a unique way that you have your own set of talents and your very own personality. Though you might not win a prize at the county fair, come in first place at a talent contest, win a full scholarship to the college of your choice, or be voted class favorite, you have some fantastic things to offer the world. They are called your personal talents -- the things you are gifted at. It can be hard work to find and use these talents, but doing so will make you feel good about yourself, if you keep your attitudes in balance.

Talents

You don't need to win a talent show to know that you're better at some things than others, or to know that you can do some things your friends or family don't want to bother with. Each of us has some special abilities that make us unique in our homes, schools, and communities. Knowing that we can do some things well shows us that we are special, and we can feel good about ourselves because of that.

As you try new things, you may discover career areas you never would have expected. Or maybe you'll just add a hobby to your life.

Art had always liked math in school, but he had no idea what he wanted to do for a career. His senior year he took courses in economics and statistics, and knew he'd found his future. While other teens had trouble working out the figures and understanding what they meant, he enjoyed it. "I never would have guessed that I'd like economics," he told his guidance counselor. "But I sure am glad you suggested that I take the course. Now I know where I want to go to college."

71

To begin to discover your own talents, take this simple test.

Here's a list that will help you get started:

Building things
Organizing trips
Playing ball
Giving parties
Windsurfing
Listening to others
Sailing
Playing an instrument
Acting
Public speaking
Running
Gardening
Sewing
Singing
Playing games
Reading
Talking
Fishing
Skiing
Doing puzzles
Skating
Working with tools
Caring for children
Teaching others
Writing
Computing

Talent Scout

1. Write down all the things you really like to do. Name things that make you feel good when you spend time at them. (*see the list, left, for help*)

2. *What comes easily to you?* Normally our talents show up in places where we have an easy time. If you like to write, you won't mind spending time at your computer, setting out stories. A friend of mine has a son who is a natural golfer. Because he enjoys it, he practices a lot.

3. *What do you spend time doing?* What activities have you been drawn to since you were a child? Perhaps you like to swim, and summertime always finds you in the water. No one has to talk you into doing it, because it just seems fun.

4. *What do people praise you for?* If you like something, you are usually going to do well in it. The more people notice and praise you, the more encouraged you will feel to continue with it.

5. *What do you dream of doing when you grow up?* Would you like to be a doctor, work with kids, be in sports, or go to another country as a missionary? If you have felt that way for a number of years, your natural talent may be drawing itself out. Because you have great skill in it, it's a logical goal.

6. *What can you practice for a long period of time?* If you hate playing the piano, chances are you'll never make it as a concert pianist. You'd end up suffering through practice, and would just have to force yourself too much. If you love it, though, you can keep at it for long enough to build your skill. Put down some things you can work at, and while it is hard work, you enjoy it and get satisfaction out of doing your best at it.

Perhaps you discovered some talents you never suspected you had. Did you find some areas I hadn't listed that make your life happier, more fun, and interesting? I hope so.

7. *Does it benefit others?* Of course you can practice lying and stealing, but that doesn't mean they should be part of your future career. Before you accept your goal, ask if it is good for you, others, and society.

Angela had almost slept through a whole year of biology. "What use do I have for this?" she wondered the whole time. But one summer, when her grandfather became ill, she offered to help her grandmother with the vegetable garden Gramps had started before he went into the hospital. "I never understood all that stuff about photosynthesis, and I don't think I could ever get a degree in science," she told her grandmother. "But I liked getting out here and watering the plants, digging the weeds, and watching the tomatoes get ripe. It was a lot of work, but next year I want Gramps to teach me how to plant my own garden, because I had so much fun." She may never own a farm or discover new kinds of plants, but Angela now has a hobby that she can share with people who need food. She also learned to can the tomatoes her family couldn't eat, and gave them to her church pantry to help homeless families in her area.

Whatever your natural talents may be, discover and make use of them. You've got your own special combination of likes and dislikes, thoughts and abilities. They have been given you as a gift for you to share with others. Once you have a direction, make the most of it.

Am I Just a Bunch of Talents?

It's fun to discover what you're good at. Knowing you can excel at things will give you a boost of enthusiasm. Yet, don't become so involved in achieving that you either place pressure on yourself to be perfect, or begin to think you are only valuable because of what you do. You own your talents – don't let them own you. You are important because of who you are and the character and integrity you live by, not just because of your talents.

Getting good grades, making it into the school play, and winning the election for class president may all be good goals, but if you are unable to achieve your goals, don't give up on yourself. When your talents become all that's important to you, you've forgotten one of the most important things in life: namely, you are loved by your family and true friends just the way you are. Even if you can't pick up a pencil, sing well enough to be in a musical, or get the vote out, you are still special.

11 Who Influences Your Feelings of You?

"It isn't where you came from, it's where you're going that counts."
– Ella Fitzgerald, singer

If self-esteem describes how you think about yourself, then where did your opinion of yourself come from? In other words, how did you get where you are today?

Many different people's opinions, and lots of experiences, went into the ideas you have about yourself. Every day the world seems to tell you where you've either failed or excelled in matters of performance, attitudes, and possessions. People may give you the feeling you are the best person in the world -- or the most unimportant.

When you hear messages about yourself, they usually come from four sources:

1. **Family attitudes.** How your family sees you and the messages they have given you about yourself.

2. **Self-imposed pressures.** Ideas of your own that compel you to take certain actions.

3. **Others' expectations.** What others think about you or what you think they think about you - that causes you to act certain ways.

4. **Hope for the future.** Your view of where you're going and how good life will be for you.

How do each of these make you feel bad or good about yourself? Let's see.

What Does My Family Tell Me?

To understand yourself, consider what you have seen day-by-day at home. The environment in which you've grown up strongly influences how you see yourself and others, because from it you learned how to handle, or avoid, problems.

- Does your family say, "I love you," easily, often, and freely? When you say it, do you really mean it?
- Does your family hug one another?
- How does your family show love? Is it hard to do that?
- When you were a child, did your mom and dad hold you in their laps, read to you, sing with you, spend time with you, and tell and show you that you were loved?
- Do you feel comfortable going to your mom and dad and talking about serious problems?
- Are your parents there for you when you share with them, or do you find it easier to hold the pain inside, because you fear their reactions?
- Do your parents seem to like another brother or sister better than you?
- Do your parents constantly compare you to a brother or sister?
- Did you feel wanted or loved during your childhood?
- Have your parents given you the feeling that they did not want you, that you were a mistake?
- Have you been abused—sexually, physically, emotionally, or verbally—by a family member or stranger?
- Does your family seem to need you?
- Do you feel truly important—that without you, your family would be less special?
- Have you helped make some family decisions?
- Would you describe your childhood as happy, sad, or painful?

Once you've answered these questions, you may have the idea that you lived in a really good home -- or one that had a lot of troubles. Understand that no matter what home life you've had, because it's all you know, it will probably seem "normal".

If you grew up in a home destroyed by alcoholism, that may seem "normal" to you, but it still won't seem right. Embarrassment makes you want to hide the fact that your mom or dad had a drinking problem. You may decide that the way to avoid sorrow is to put on a happy face, becoming everyone's favorite comedian while you hide your hurt inside.

On the other hand, if you grew up in a family that expressed love easily and went through tough times together, you may not understand what the problem is with other families. You'll expect everyone to have a family as "normal" as yours, and you may find it hard to understand why other teens seem to think they aren't valuable to their parents, brothers, and/or sisters.

If you have a good family life, be very thankful for it. Your parents weren't perfect, but they gave you a warm home. Do all you can to make your family even better. Then reach out and share your love with others.

If you come from a home that lacked love, take heart. Freedom comes when you realize that you cannot control your family situation. You cannot change your parents' mistakes, and you had nothing to do with any pain they inflicted upon you. Refuse to carry the blame and guilt. Instead, begin to take control of your life, where possible.

If you feel depressed all the time, instead of suffering through the "down" times that come with specific problems, seek out a trained counselor who can help you understand your feelings and share with you ways to rebuild your life by dealing with the pain and moving forward.

Sarah told me about her experience with her jealous mother. This teen could hardly go out of the house without hearing her mother's complaints follow her out the door. Sarah never got in trouble when she left home; she simply wanted to spend a little time with friends. Because she had never done anything to cause her mother to be worried, Sarah didn't understand her mother's behavior.

As it turned out, the problem did not lie with Sarah, but with her mother. Mrs. Montrose had married at sixteen, and her marriage had ended in divorce. Now Sarah was sixteen, too, and her mother was reacting in anger. When she looked at the teen, she blamed her daughter for her own missed-out-on childhood, the lost opportunity for a college education, and all the other things that an early marriage had denied her. Though she didn't realize it consciously, Mrs. Montrose kept Sarah at home so she would not get pregnant, too.

Sadly, Mrs. Montrose will not accept help for her concealed pain; she resists change. Fortunately, that does not mean Sarah has no hope. Instead of running away from home to get rid of these problems, Sarah has wisely decided to stay for a few more years. Though she cannot change the problems, she has altered the way she thinks about them. Sarah cares for her mother -- even when she plays mind tricks on Sarah -- but this teen does not buy into the hurt anymore.

"I understand that you are hurting," she told her mother. "But I am not responsible for what happened before I was born. If you need help, I'll provide any that I can, but I also have my own life." She went on to convince her mom that she would not get pregnant; instead she planned on making the right choices. Realizing the influence her mother's poor self-image had on her view of herself, Sarah began to change her thought patterns, and carved out her own successful junior and senior years.

Family has a powerful influence on you, but it does not have the last word. Love them, even when it seems hard, but don't let your parents, brothers, or sisters manipulate you or put you down.

How Do I Pressure Myself?

Though we often don't have much control over our family situations, we do have total say in the pressures we put on ourselves. It's up to us if we'll become reactors, who only go with the flow, or initiators, who make things happen. Do you value what's good and right for you, or do you make yourself do what you think others want?

Susie's father was very unhappy with his marriage, so he avoided arguments by never spending time at home. To build up his hurting self-esteem, he did more than the next guy at work. That meant he spent many hours in the office, and few with Susie. He built his life on the good opinion of his boss, and avoided getting close to his family.

When Susie started dating, at thirteen, she did not have a good relationship model to build on, so she did what "everyone" did. By sixteen she had already had four boyfriends, each only after sex.

Deep down, Susie knew her boyfriends did not love her.

"Why do you do it, then?" I asked.

"It may not be right for me to have sex with them, and I know it won't last forever, but night after night, year after year, I've wanted my father to let me know that he loved me," she shared. "When my boyfriends put their arms around me and say they love me, at least it's something. Maybe no one can stop the pain, but at least I forget for a while."

Even the fear that she was pregnant -- several times -- did not keep Susie from having sex. When one boy abandoned her, she simply went on to the next.

I could see that Susie had a sad future ahead if she did not change her course. So I helped her understand that the path she had taken would never heal the pain. "You can stop this kind of behavior if you want to," I counseled.

"I could never do it," she cried. "You don't know what I feel inside!"

"What would you do if a boy came up and tried to force you to have sex with him?" I asked.

"I'd yell so loudly you'd hear me from here to the next county," Susie answered quickly and proudly. "That'd only be the beginning -- I'd kick, claw, and punch until he left me alone."

"Well, it's the same thing here. Once you decide that the short-term gain of having sex is not worth it, you'll fight just as hard to avoid it."

Susie had to understand how her family had influenced her, and that she didn't have to look for love in sex before marriage, which would only bring her pain. The pressure to have a boyfriend stemmed from her fear that others might think she couldn't attract anyone. Her imagination concerning what others thought gave her a warped picture of the truth. No one really thought the things she imagined. She had pressured herself into it. Once she understood her mistake, she could learn to love herself enough to say no. She could become an initiator.

Not everyone does drugs or has sex to try to be happy.

Bob spent his childhood trying to earn his dad's approval by getting top grades. Because he had to study so hard, he never got the chance to go out for the basketball team or learn to play the trumpet really well. All his efforts went into getting A's so that he could hear his dad sing his praises to his friends.

I met Bob when he was twenty-two. He had made it into a fine law school, and though he talked about how proud his dad was of him, Bob appeared depressed. His face had no life in it, and his eyes seemed dull. The very thing he'd done to please his dad had ruined his own feelings about himself.

I showed Bob that he'd actually pressured himself into doing something he hated because he thought he had to have his father's approval. He had never stood his ground with his dad and shared his own desires.

Bob decided to talk to his school counselor about changing to another program. Then he would speak to his dad and explain that he had only tried to be a lawyer to please him. I pray his dad understood and loved him as he was.

You need unconditional love -- love that supports you when you're in trouble or when things are going well. Ideally, you should find that in your home, but not every family has learned the skills that make such love possible.

If your parents can't love you without reservation, tap into some unconditional love in your church, through friends, and perhaps through a counselor who can help heal the hurts. Don't stay out in the cold. Take control of those self-imposed pressures by understanding where you are coming from, how your situation has caused you to move in some poor directions, and how you can change that. Create a step-by-step program for a new life by turning bad habits into good ones.

As you take charge of life, you'll build up your opinion of yourself. Even if you're not facing a real crisis today, you can start by making a few good habits part of your daily routine:

Healthy Self-esteem Habits

These are some of my daily habits:

1. Get plenty of sleep to be at your best each morning
2. Eat right so you don't feel grouchy
3. Exercise regularly so you look and feel good
4. Read something encouraging and uplifting so you won't focus on problems and troubles

I find that once I start forgetting to keep these good habits going, I start forming bad ones: I start to believe I'm not a good speaker if someone has to call and cancel; if I overhear someone saying something about me, I take it the wrong way; and I begin to get depressed -- over nothing!

We all can make a decision to develop self-esteem by thinking thoughts and taking actions that make us positive, happy, whole, and real. Like athletes who spend many hours practicing skills, training, and staying in shape, we have to strengthen our own self-esteem.

We can't do that by putting wrongful pressure upon ourselves and giving up easily when we face the need to change.

What Do I Think Others Think?

Not long ago seventeen-year-old Jim wrote to me:

Dear Bill:

I've recently heard you speak and started to do many of the things you mentioned like, treat myself with respect, treat others the way I want to be treated and put more effort into my schoolwork and family. I'm really glad you sent me the book to help me grow and become more positive in my outlook on life.

But there is still pain in my heart. I don't feel great, the way I thought I would after doing many of the things you said would help. I still have a problem. At my school, if you have a girlfriend, you have it made-you can go places and do things with the crowd. I don't have a girlfriend. Though I want one girl to like me, she never looks at me.

What can I do to get her to like me? I've asked her out, but she will not go. At night I cry and get so depressed that I want to die. I know I'm in love with her because I feel so strongly in my heart-I know it's real.

Last year I had a girlfriend and felt wonderful, but she dumped me for another guy. I felt so bad I couldn't believe it; it took me six months to get over her. Now that I'm finally in love with another girl, she will not have a thing to do with me.

Please help me. What should I do?

Jim

When I wrote back to Jim, I pointed out that he was acting as if this girl would take care of all his problems. In his mind, he was trying to live up to the expectations of what people in his school thought. So, he thought he could only feel good about himself if a girl had his ring. If he had to walk through the halls alone, he told himself he was insignificant and worthless. Instead of finding other guys who were not dating, and hanging out with them, he gave up.

Maybe you've heard the saying, "I'm not who I think I am. I'm not who you think I am. But I am who I think you think I am."

Do you:

- Do what you think you should or what you think others think you should?
- Feel good when you do what is right or try to please others, no matter what?
- Ask yourself, "Will my friends approve?" before you make a decision?
- Wear only clothes that you are sure no one would ever laugh at?
- Only wear jewelry others will think is awesome?
- Go places you hate because others expect you to go there?
- Fear wearing your seat belt, because your friends would think you were weird?
- Do less than your best when you study for tests, because you might get better grades than a friend?
- Quit a team because one of your friends is kicked off?
- Look around before asking a question in class?
- Fear helping another student pick up their spilled books because you might look stupid?
- Stay and listen to dirty jokes because others are?

Don't live up to the expectations of others if those ideas are less than the best for you. Darla had a chance at being first-chair flute in the band, but she gave it up to run away with a friend. When she came back in six months, she couldn't make it in the band again. Regret for that mistake lasts, even though it happened long ago.

A few years after you graduate high school, you probably won't even know the people whose opinions mean so much to you today. Though I graduated with several hundred others, I have only kept in touch with one -- my best friend, Steve McKinley -- and we only see each other a few times a year.

Today I can't remember the names of the teens who encouraged me to do things I later regretted. I only remember the pain. In college, another student asked if I could take a test for him. At first I said no, but I agreed to do it when he persisted. The professor found us out, and we both got kicked out of the class and received zeros for the entire semester. Not only did it affect my grade-point average, but on my record are the words "Expelled for cheating". Twenty years later, I can't remember the other boy's name, but I still bear the scars for what I did.

Start to really live today by doing what is right, not what feels good, what everyone else says you should, or what others are doing. You know deep in your heart what is right and what is wrong. Make every decision count, **starting with you, starting today**.

If everyone else wants to keep on doing wrong, you may not have the power to change that. Just leave. You live in America, a free country. You can go where you want, do what you want, become what you want. All of that starts today.

Are you a girl who will sit through any kind of movie your boyfriend wants to see? Maybe you need to assert your own opinion. Are you a boy who is to shy to walk out of the movie if what you see and hear is offensive to you? Maybe you need to summon up some courage and say to your date, "Come on, I am getting my money back."

I do not take my wife to R-rated movies, because she is too special. You, too, are valuable. Don't treat yourself as if you weren't, and don't let friends or family take advantage of you by leading you into actions that you can't feel proud of. Stand up for yourself firmly but kindly. As they see your strength, others will respect you, even if they give you trouble at first.

Choices for Success or Failure

Do you follow the crowd or do the good, right thing?

Will you:

- Avoid negative TV programs
- Say, "I love you," to your parents
- Treat your family with respect

- Sit next to the "class nerd"
- Make others smile on a dark day
- Thank people for the things they've done for you
- Tell a teacher her class was exciting
- Break off bad relationships
- Choose friends who will challenge you to do your best
- Call a friend and thank him for being there for you
- Challenge your classmates to do the right things

Or do you:

- Listen to the most popular radio station - bad message and all
- Avoid your parents as much as you can
- Dump on your brothers and sisters
- Make fun of the kid next to you in homeroom
- Complain that nothing ever goes right for you
- Get into as much trouble as you can with your friends
- Avoid unpopular kids as much as possible
- Feel that everything in your life revolves around being accepted by the 'in crowd' at school

Living up to the expectations of others, when you know those ideas are wrong or just not right for you, can make you very sorry. If a friend offers advice, listen; think about it, but don't blindly follow. When your dad talks to you about your future, follow his guidance, but make certain he knows what your talents and best attributes are. Decide together if the road he is suggesting is best suited for you.

Do I Have Hope for the Future?

When you look toward the future, what do you expect? How you answer that question will influence how you feel about yourself.

Do you feel:

- Trapped, locked into your past
- Upbeat, knowing you are prepared to do your best in the future
- Doubtful about how you can handle life

- Listless, because you have no goals
- Excited, because you can see where you're going tomorrow
- Sad, since you can see trouble down the road

Sometimes we all feel as if we haven't a clue about where to go next. When we face hard times, doubt may drag us down. That's why it's important to have a goal in life. When you have plans and purpose, you'll walk around school with a step that's brisk, with an attitude that says, "I can do this," and with hope for tomorrow.

People ask me, "What keeps you speaking in schools? Don't you know that half the kids in the seats don't want to be there anyway? Why don't you just throw in the towel?"

"I can't give up," I answer, "because one of those kids is Billy Sanders. He will not listen unless I give every ounce of energy I've got. I have to show him I really love him and that I believe in what I say, even if his school doesn't want to hear it. Otherwise, I may miss and lose this kid forever. He may never come back." I have hope for the future of each teen I speak to.

I don't want any teen to be like the one I heard about when a classmate wrote me:

Dear Bill:

The night you spoke to the parents at my school, a boy committed suicide by hanging himself. The sad thing is, he skipped out of school the day you spoke and never heard a word of your assembly. He never heard how you overcame your problems and that he could do it, too.

Bill, I believe that he would be alive today if he had heard you. I'm sorry he wasn't there, but for those who are in your next assembly, never stop saying what you are saying.

With love,

Sherry

I share Sherry's sadness at the loss of that boy, but her letter gives me a picture of just why I speak to teens. When some of them don't listen, I can still put all my love and compassion into reaching out, because I picture that boy who missed my words.

Do you have:

- Things to look forward to?
- People's lives to touch?
- Goals to reach?
- Blessings to impart?
- Hope for the future?

Without hope, we turn to dope. Without hope, we sometimes grope. Without hope, many kids smoke. Without hope, some kids toke. Without hope, our lives are choked.

I hope you have hope, but if you don't, you can get it. Don't give up, because then you really have lost out. As long as you're working on building hope, you'll have a chance for a better tomorrow. I believe in you, and so do so many others in your life. You have what it takes to make it through school and in life. Believe in yourself, your abilities, your future. You do have things to look forward to, but first you must set your sights on them. You so have people's lives to touch, but first you have to take your eyes off of yourself and how good you look walking down the halls of your school. You have many fine goals to reach, but you have to be the one to set them. Blessings are waiting inside you to be passed on to others. Your future is ahead of you. Build hope inside of you. Then you will have hope for the future. Get going; it's really going to be great!

12 The Harm In Following the Crowd

"I don't know the key to success, but the key to failure is trying to please everbody."
– Bill Cosby, comedian

In order to make great decisions and become someone others can rightfully admire, you must first develop insight and foresight into the people you hang around with. Even more important, you must understand who it is that influences and leads you. Many guys and girls have been led down the wrong path by their so-called, "best friends". Many girls have had their lives ruined by the boyfriend who wanted sex, but talked of love; just as many guys have followed their friends in a wild night of "fun" that resulted in their doing something they regretted the rest of their lives.

As you go through these next few chapters, try and identify the individuals who are in your life, but who don't have your best interest at hand. These are the people who are causing you to do more negative things than you are influencing them to do positive, healthy activities.

Harmful peer pressure is very real. You feel it every day when someone gives you messages like these:

- To be in with the "right" crowd you have to do drugs.
- Cheating is okay. After all, even the teachers expect it.
- Getting good grades means you are a "Goody Two-Shoes".
- Spending time with your family is dumb. They aren't important.
- No one likes teachers. They just don't count.
- Cool people don't ask questions in class.

- Don't worry about doing what's right. Have some fun. Don't be old-fashioned by believing that stuff.
- Prove you really love me by having sex with me-I'm using protection.

The list could go on and on.

Whenever you either do something wrong, or don't do something good because you are afraid of what others will think or do, you are a victim of negative peer pressure. In such cases, you have let yourself become a captive to what others think, meaning you're unable to think for yourself and seek the best goals for your own life.

What Price Are You Paying?

Most people assume that, at some point, you have to give in to negative pressure in order to be "normal", "fit in", or be "popular". I disagree. Too often I've seen teens give in to the pressures of so-called friends -- and paid a heavy price. Look at some of the hurt peer pressure can cause:

- Chet didn't want his friends to think he was too smart, so he didn't do his best on tests. When it came time to apply to college, he couldn't make it into the school of his choice.

- Kyle stole a ten-dollar cassette, and by doing so, he landed himself in a juvenile home for a year-and-a-half.

- Richard got drunk at a party. His friends told him to have sex with a girl at the party. Today she's pregnant with his child, and he hardly even knows her.

- Sharon didn't even like booze. Her parents were alcoholics, and she knew where drinking could lead. But when her friends wanted to drink at a party, she went along with it. Every time she drinks now, she does something stupid and hurts someone.

- Marcy is only eighteen, and has already had two abortions. Now she has nightmares, and can't forget how she took the lives of her babies. When she gave in to her boyfriends' pressure to abort the children, she never knew about the pain she'd feel today.

Being part of the crowd will never make you a leader in your school, a person people remember with pride, or a future success. It could, however, cause you a lot of heartache and leave you with many regrets. That's why I want to give you some tools that will help you to both identify negative pressure and avoid its consequences.

Your Negative Pressure Toolbox

When you face a decision and need to know if you are looking at negative pressure, ask yourself the following six questions:

1. *Is it based on truth?* Peer pressure is often based on lies or false assumptions. Many times students stay in cliques that are bad for them simply because the leader of a group has convinced them that if they go against the group, they will lose all of their friends. In other cases, girls have sex because they confuse lust and excited hormones with love.

    The truth, however, will not cause you harm in the long run. It will not sway you to make a decision that will bring you pain forever, and it will not distort what is real.

    When you don't follow the crowd, you can often be confident you are following the truth. Going the opposite way of most people might even make you a leader. Yet, even if it doesn't, living up to what is right, honest, and good, will at least help you to feel positive about yourself.

2. *Would I do this if my parents or a teacher were here?* The fact is, you have to live with yourself all the time. But if you knew your parents could see you right now, would you do this thing? Would you drink that? Would you go to this place? If the answer is no,

91

you can be sure you are making a poor decision.

Feeling bad about your behavior can be a very healthy reaction. It can keep you from doing wrong or repeating a mistake. Make use of this warning system in your life.

3. *Do I feel good about myself after I do this?* I frequently hear from teens about how awful they feel after they've had sex and their boyfriends are gone; or how terrible they feel after they've used drugs or drunk the booze.

   Minimize regrets in your life by not repeating the mistakes that cause them. If it's wrong, don't do it.

4. Would I want this activity written up in the newspaper? If everyone could read about what you've done, would you feel good, or miserable? Answering this question truthfully could eliminate many things from your plans.

   While you try new things and seek excitement, be careful that you will not regret your fun. Don't do wrong just because it is popular and common. You are too special to make that mistake.

5. *Does this activity show true concern for others?* Selfish activities will not make you a better person. Anyone who wants to merely take, take, take, shows little concern for you and will not improve your life. You do not need such friends. Avoid people who want to gossip, put others down, or have a level of anger that is passed on to others. In your own actions, make certain you help others, reach out to hurting people, and think about how what you say could hurt or help them.

6. *Would my future be better if I did this?* When I speak at schools, I ask teens to name someone who used

alcohol, and improved his life from that use. No one has given me a good answer to my question. Alcohol has never bettered a person. It only tears down dreams, futures, families, and hopes. In other words, it only makes people worse. Drinking can never brighten your future.

Then I ask teens to name someone whose premarital or extramarital sex has improved his or her life. No one can give me an answer for that either.

I have poured my life into this book, and I want you to find the truth about your life through it. Please don't take the easy road out. Walk the path that is seldom walked: the one that has brush on it and that few people go down. It is a narrow path, but it is exciting and wonderful -- as well as tough. You have to stand up in order to see over the branches and see that there is a light at the end of this path. Though few will travel it, you can be one of those few.

To that end, write the following five questions on a 3 x 5 card, and put the card where you'll see it everyday. When you have asked these questions, you can also ask yourself, *What are the consequences of this for me?*

1. Could this activity kill me?
2. Could it ruin my dreams?
3. Could it tarnish my feelings about myself?
4. Could I lose the respect of others?
5. Could I hurt my reputation?

If you answered yes to any of those questions, the activity you are being pressured to do is not worth it. Though you may avoid paying the price of such an activity in the short run, you are going to pay eventually. It isn't over till it's over. When you know a super stud who has sex with every girl he can get his hands on, you may not know, for example, that he has AIDS – that is, until ten years later. (And if he is fortunate enough to not get AIDS, he'll be haunted by the memories of all his past sex partners every time he has sex with his wife.) Likewise, someone who speeds may not get caught today, but one day he may either lose his life in an accident or spend his life in a nursing home because the doctors can't fix the damage the accident did to his body. Look beyond the fun of today to the future you have tomorrow.

Peer pressure isn't just what happens to you; you may do it every day to others.

Don't Be Part of the Problem

You have felt the sting of negative pressure. People have tried to make you do things their way, go along with what's wrong to make them feel right, or follow their leadership when they didn't have your best interests at heart. But maybe you have also led others to do wrong by pressuring them.

"I really messed up!" Len admitted. "Just after I met John, I insisted that my friend, Tom, hang around with him, too. John was new to our school, and I thought he needed friends.

"After a few days, Tom pointed out that John wasn't very honest. When our math teacher gave a quiz, John hadn't studied, so he wanted to see Tom's answers before he handed in his paper. I thought it would only happen once, and I told Tom not to make too much of it.

"Tom didn't say a lot about John after that. They weren't close. But when we went out, the three of us usually went together.

"Tom's brother, Stu, came with us a few times. He and John really hit it off. Until later I didn't find out that there was a lot more about John that I didn't know. He was involved with a car-theft ring, and he was looking for more kids to get involved. From the start, he'd known that Tom and I wouldn't go for it, but he knew he could meet people through us.

"Stu got involved in the ring and got into a lot of trouble. How I wish I'd listened to Tom and never insisted that they stay friends!"

Pressuring people can lead to plenty of trouble. Len didn't intend to hurt anyone -- he only wanted to help a new teen in his school. But in his "love me, love my friend" attitude toward Tom, he was exerting peer pressure on his friend.

Peer pressure isn't just what happens to you; you may do it everyday to others as well. How do you feel in the following circumstances?

- In a conversation, people do not see things your way.
- You and your friends don't dress in the same styles.
- Your friends go places with people who aren't your friends.
- Your group doesn't get involved in all your after school activities.

Do any of these situations make you feel uncomfortable? When you feel this way, what do you do? Do you push your best friend to join your team, even when he doesn't want to? Do you make fun of someone who doesn't wear the latest fashions? If so, you are pressuring them to do things your way. It's a form of bullying.

Everyone pressures other people at some time. Often it's a passive pressure to agree, join in, or have fun. Sometimes we get mad when others don't do things our way or see eye to eye with us. As much as possible, we need to understand that other people are individuals too. We should be sensitive to our friends' needs to do things their own way, get involved in ideas and activities that can help them for the future, and become the best people they can be.

As long as your friends are moving forward -- doing the things that will improve their futures -- don't pressure them to follow your personal path. It's when you see them making mistakes that can hurt their lives that you need to both lovingly confront them and gently pressure them to do the good things that will build their lives.

Remember, some of the people who pressure you may actually have your good at heart. Make the pressure you put on others' lives the kind they will thank you for in the end. Stand up for others because they too are worth it.

"Later, I found out that Tom stuck with me because he did not want John to hurt my life," Len shared. "When I found that out, I felt so humbled. Tom and I are working now to help Stu out of his trouble. I feel as if it's my fault he met John, and I want to help him find better friends."

Checkpoints

Review or discuss this chapter using the fol-lowing questions.

1. What is negative peer pressure?

2. What are some questions you can ask yourself when you face negative pressure? Which ones would be most effective for you?

3. What five questions will help you identify the consequences of giving in to a specific pressure?

4. How have you exerted negative peer pressure on someone? What was the result?

13 Taking the Harm out of Peer Pressure

"The ugly reality is that peer pressure reaches its greatest intensity at just the age when kids tend to be most insensitive and cruel".

– Walt Mueller, "Understanding Today's Youth Culture"

Peer pressure can hurt, but it doesn't have to. That's why I want to share this simple, four-step strategy that will help take the sting out of it. The strategy is summed up by four words: perception, planning, people, and purpose.

Perception, Planning, People, Purpose

With these four words, you can chart a course that will help enable you to avoid the stumbling blocks that other people, your own lack of understanding, or your own wrong choices could be putting in the way of a successful voyage through life.

Peer Pressure Quiz

Please answer "yes" or "no" to the following questions. There are no right or wrong answers. Simply identify where you are now so you can more clearly see where you want to go in the future.

Do you wear the clothes you wear because you think others will approve?

Do you keep from wearing clothing that you know is different from the trends, or something that will surely get others' attention?

Is your hairstyle "in"?

If your hairstylist wanted to experiment on you, would you say no?

If it were Fifties Day at your school, would you be too embarrassed to slick your hair back or wear a ponytail and white socks?

Have you ever held back from trying to get top grades because the people you hang around with would not be comfortable?

Have you ever joined in with others as they were "putting down" or laughing at another student?

Would it be difficult for you to either stop a fight or tell others not to pick on a certain student?

Do you keep from wearing your seatbelt when someone else drives?

Even if you wear your seatbelt when you ride in a car, do you ever hold back from asking others to wear theirs?

Do you feel a strong need to go to college or get into a certain profession because "significant others" expect you to?

Is it hard for you to approach your parents and discuss how you disagree with their expectations of you?

Do you avoid showing affection to a family member while you are around other students?

Do you avoid saying "I love you" to a family member or a close friend?

If you wore braces, would it be hard for you to smile?

Do you feel embarrassed if others snicker at one of your questions in class?

Is it hard for you to ask disruptive students to be quiet during class?

Do you go to parties at which you feel uncomfortable?

At parties do you ever do things you don't believe in?

Do you watch or listen to TV programs, movies, and "in" music even though you don't agree with the message being expressed?

Would it be hard for you to walk out of a movie if you were offended -- even if you were with a group of friends?

Do you avoid sitting in a different place with different students in the cafeteria?

Have you ever wanted to go out for a sport or school play, but did not?

Do you steal things or cheat on tests because a friend does?

Do you lie because your friends expect you to?

Is it hard for you to go to your parent(s) with your problems and concerns?

Have you ever had a great idea, but felt ashamed to tell anyone or share it in class?

Do you often disagree with your teacher, but never say anything?

Have you ever felt like complimenting your teacher, but didn't?

Is it hard for you to arrive early and stay later and work harder than other employees at the place where you work?

Do you avoid praying before meals when you are out with friends?

Are you afraid to share your religious convictions with other people, even if they ask?

Would it be hard for you to stay after practice (for any sport) and work out, even if others scoffed at you?

Is it difficult for you to tell a friend, "I am going to stay home tonight and work on my term paper"?

If you knew someone was ruining his life with drugs, would it be a tough decision for you to get him the help he needs?

Would it be tough for you to go to a party and drink a Dr. Pepper if you knew everyone else was drinking alcohol and would make fun of you?

If several students were leaving a party totally "blitzed", would it be embarrassing for you to persuade them not to drive, but to ride with you?

If a fellow student had a real emptiness in her heart and she felt she had nothing to live for, would you find it difficult to get her in touch with a counselor?

If you saw your boss stealing from the company you work for, would you confront him or her?

Is it almost impossible for you to invite a younger brother or sister to do something with you at a place where you will be seen by your peers?

(Given by permission by Bill Sanders, Tuff Turf, Fleming Revel publishers.)

Scoring Procedure

Add up the number of your "Yes" responses to the above questions. A score of 25 or more indicates you are a person more deeply affected by peer pressure. A score between 10 and 25 indicates peer pressure may affect you, but not very much. A score between 0 and 10 indicates that you probably have a great deal of self-confidence (that is, if you answered the questions honestly).

Are you seeing yourself and others clearly or does peer pressure cloud your vision?

Perception

Each of us sees things differently. Our perception is our reality.

"I thought it would all turn out right," Mary cried to me during a counseling session, after I had spent two days at her large high school. "I thought he loved me, and I believed he had my best interests at heart. When he said that someday we would marry and it was okay to have sex now, I accepted that. He said I'd never regret it, but I do." The tears streamed down her face.

Mary thought she'd made the right decision. David, her boyfriend, had seemed like a caring person who would always look out for her, but now that her senior year was ending, Mary discovered he wouldn't be part of her future. Where had she gone wrong?

Mary had the wrong perception of the situation. She saw sex as being okay – considering the circumstances – but the problem was that the circumstances had changed. Although David initially seemed to care about her, once she had sex with him their relationship lost the challenge he needed. He saw her as conquered, and he looked for someone new.

How we perceive things has a lot to do with how we act. I have met some convicts who told me they never thought they would get caught, and others who had convinced themselves they'd done nothing wrong. Their ideas could not have been more mistaken -- and prison came as a great shock to them.

How do you perceive yourself and others? The answer to that question will influence your choices. Are you seeing clearly, or does peer pressure cloud your vision? Do you fear what other people might say about you, or do to you if you don't follow the popular idea of the moment? That negative perception will not lead to what's best for you. Do you have to agree with your friends in order to have stature? Then you'll go along with others because you want to feel good about yourself. But following the crowd will not give you the results you expect. Do you do it because you think others will admire you? If so, you are wrong! No one looks up to a follower who never makes his or her own choices. Making your own decisions, based on clear thinking, will eventually gain you much more admiration.

When you look at yourself, do you see a special, valued person? Unless you envision yourself that way, you will not avoid the things that destroy you.

"I can't have that attitude," Doug objected. "It makes me sound as if I thought I was better than anyone else, and I've been taught that I'm supposed to be humble."

I'm not suggesting that you get a swelled head, just that you know of your ultimate worth. Doug's wrong because valuing yourself as the special person you are has nothing to do with pride or humility. You don't have to go around bragging about your talents; it's simply a matter of believing that you were made as a loving, caring, awesome person.

Planning

Step one is to see yourself as your family and close friends see you. You are awesome and full of potential. This book will work very hard to convince you of your worth – to yourself, your family and loved ones, and to those lives you were sent to make a difference in.

Step two is making a plan that will help you make the right choices. Failure to plan leads to failure.

Whenever I talk to teens in trouble, over and over again I learn that they made the same mistake: they never had a plan. Since they didn't know where they were going, they followed the crowd. At the last moment, they always agreed to do what others wanted, even if they didn't know what would happen. In the end, they were sorry -- after it was too late.

One stupid party ruined Jim's entire sophomore year -- and may influence his whole life. He got drunk, and when someone offered him marijuana, it sounded like a good idea.

"Until we got caught, that is," he admitted. "I got kicked off the team, and it ruined my chance at college. I'd wanted a sports scholarship, but that one night probably ruined it. It didn't make any difference that I'd never used drugs before -- they caught me in the act."

Today Jim knows that he could have avoided that mistake by simply having had a plan not to go to parties where there were drugs and booze. "Tell other teens how important it is to think ahead," he said, "so they don't end up in my position."

The basic steps for making a plan are:

Step 1: Try to verbalize the types of peer pressure you might encounter. Write down the things that concern you, being as specific as possible.

Step 2: Think about all the possible ways you could respond to the pressures.

Step 3: Discuss these answers with someone you respect (usually someone older and wiser).

Step 4: Decide on the best response for each pressure, and commit yourself to it.

Step 5: Talk to one or two good friends who will support you in your commitment.

Step 6: Ask for others' help in keeping your commitment.

Failure to plan leads to failure.

Without a plan, you could end up in Jim's shoes. But by having a plan that identifies trouble spots, you can skirt a lot of problems in life. The next two chapters will help you develop positive plans that can impact your life – and the lives of others.

People

The next step is choosing to be around people who will not hinder your effort to make good choices.

How do you choose the people you want to hang around? Perhaps you look for the coolest crowd in school, or date the guys who most annoy your parents. Remember, you usually become like the people who have the most influence on you: friends, family, and co-workers. Chances are also very good that they will influence you more than you influence them. This is especially true when you become part of a crowd.

Recently, Susan shared her story with me. "When I joined the drama club, I thought I would have a real impact on what was going on. Even though I knew they were hard on people, gossiped all the time and used profanity in every other sentence, I thought that by being a good example when I was with them would make a difference.

"I wish it had worked that way. I didn't change them but through it all I've learned you can't change anyone but yourself. Even though they didn't stop with their verbal abuse on others, they did tone it down when I was there. One time, a couple of them even apologized to me about someone's foul language. I look at it as a small accomplishment. At least they didn't influence me."

I'm proud of Susan. She was trying to do what is almost impossible unless you are extremely strong in your own values. People can make you do things you'd never think of doing otherwise: they can distract you so that you make mistakes, and make you doubt what you value.

That's why parents and teens often disagree about friends. Mom and dad may, for example, want you to spend time with someone you can't stand, while objecting to your best friend. Why? Because they want the best for you, and they know that if you're not careful, you could be influenced in harmful ways. When you bring home friends, your parents can usually tell when they are trouble. Because they have more experience with people, they can see when a girlfriend is spoiled and wants her own way, or when a boyfriend will try to push you around. Parents can often spot character problems that teens miss. So ask your parents what they think, and take their advice when they see trouble ahead. It could save you a lot of pain.

People have an important role in helping you avoid negative peer pressure and making good decisions. We've already identified the positive and negative people in your life. The next few chapters will help you harness positive pressure and make it work for you.

Purpose

Do you have a purpose in life, or are you just wandering through? Plans help you with the day-to-day choices, but you need to develop a broader purpose, too. Where do you want to be five years from now, ten years from now, and at the end of your life? Who can help you get to your goal, and what action do you need to take today to get there?

You may not hit all your goals, but a larger purpose in life will keep you from sweating the small stuff and help you avoid a lot of problems.

Jeff was a high school honor-roll student who wanted to become a doctor. "Sure, I could have gone to more parties, spent more time with friends, and gone to the shore more," he said. "But I knew that putting time into those and avoiding studying would never get me into a good college. If I didn't go to a top-notch college, I couldn't get into the best medical school. So I was willing to give up some weekend plans for my future.

"I just got accepted into an Ivy League school. If I keep my goals in sight, I can make my plans come true. Now all the parties I missed don't mean a thing."

Jeff has a goal that will take a lot of work, but he's also developing the self-control and study habits that can make him successful in his chosen field. Every step of the way is important, so today he's making the decisions that will help his career.

Perhaps you hate science and could never become a doctor. That doesn't mean you can't make decisions today that will help fulfill your purpose for tomorrow. You do it every time you:

- Avoid drugs because you only have one brain – and it needs to last a lifetime.
- Choose after-school activities that will build your skills and help you learn teamwork.

- Make friends you can be proud of.
- Read stuff that is positive and helpful, and not degrading or dirty.
- Spend time with your family, even though peers tell you that parents are uncool.
- Challenge a friend who is stealing, because you care for his future more than you care what people will say.
- Say no to sex because your life and future marriage are too important to put at risk.

Discover where you want to be in the future, and start planning for it today. This could change your entire life.

If you don't like what's happening in certain areas of your life, you need to make a plan and make some changes.

Checkpoints

Review or discuss this chapter using the following questions:

1. What is perception? How does it influence the decisions you make?

2. What do your family and loved ones have to say about you? How should this give you a positive view of yourself?

3. How does planning help you avoid mistakes and make better decisions?

4. How do people influence the choices you make? How do you decide which people you want to be with?

5. What purpose do you have in life? Do you need to develop new goals and plans?

14 Following in Others' Footsteps

"A friend is someone who knows the song in your heart and can sing it back to you when you have forgotten the words".

– Anonymous

Whether or not we realize it, we all follow somebody. Maybe it's another teen who dresses in the latest styles, or an adult who has accomplished something you aspire to. Or maybe you follow someone else entirely. But the question is not, "Are you following someone?"; it's "Who are you following?"

Who Do You Follow?

When you look around your school, your town, or your church, do you see people you admire? Do you follow them? Do you imitate people who have worthy goals? Or, do you just follow a short-term friend down an easy path?

I'm not asking these questions idly. Many teens write to tell me about their poor leadership choices. Many more are forced to live with the consequences of a poor decision -- perhaps for the rest of their lives. Too often, these teens have made a decision in the heat of the moment that they'd like to undo today.

"I thought Chuck was in love with me," Mary wrote. "'He'd never do anything to harm me,' I thought. But that was before I found out I was pregnant. Just after I broke the news to him, he dumped me. I can't tell you how alone I feel at a time when I have to make a huge decision about the life growing inside me. I feel as if I've been used, and that's just what I think Chuck did to me."

Mary isn't the only person to be led astray by a guy. Girls often make poor decisions under the influence of a guy; and many guys start down the wrong path under a girl's influence. But it needn't be a member of the opposite sex. Bad influences come in every shape, size, and sex.

Recently I spoke to some gang members. Their leader promised that fame, power, and money would be theirs if they followed him. It was all a lie, as Micky discovered when he landed in jail because he followed the wrong leader.

Where Do You Follow?

Though most of us like to think of ourselves as being pretty independent, the truth is we all have a deep need for someone we can look up to. If we have a hard time finding a true leader, we may settle for one that isn't so good.

Such a man made the news a while ago. His name was David Koresh, and he led dozens of people to their deaths. People who were desperately seeking someone to tell them what to do, what to think, how to dress, how to act, and what to believe in, gave their lives for a man who led them astray.

Yet, you don't have to follow a cult leader to be led down a wrong path. Sometimes you need only turn on the TV or pop in a compact disc. Subtle (and not-so-subtle) media messages capture the minds of people of all ages. In fact, I think the media get away with pushing some of their bad ideas because we all have forgotten how to think, how to be the masters of our own destiny.

That easy trap of a go-with-the-flow mentality is why I encourage people to carefully choose who they will follow. Sure, it's simpler to allow leaders to make decisions for you -- much easier than choosing your own plan of action -- but it can be deadly.

Choosing a Leader

Before you follow someone, take the time to check him or her out.

Boldness and confidence are not the only elements that make up a leader, so before you follow someone, know what they actually stand for. Look a little deeper than the outside -- search for his values. That way you will know how he is likely to act, and will be able to foresee the things that will motivate him.

In Wichita, Kansas, I met the kind of leader teens can follow with confidence. Her name is Cheryl Hurley, and she is in charge of an organization called High School Ministry Network.

Cheryl is a woman who has known the sting of pain. She went through a difficult divorce, and her daughter ran away.

Cheryl now has the desire, love, and vision to reach out to teens. She wants to change hurting lives, and to that end she took charge of eighteen leadership classes, all in different high schools.

Recently, Cheryl brought me into one of the toughest high schools in Wichita. Prominent signs hopefully proclaimed, "Drug-Free School Zone" and "Gun-Free School Zone". Guards were posted at every entrance.

It took the students several minutes to settle down before I could be introduced. I had been told that even if I only spoke twenty minutes, they would appreciate whatever I could communicate to the teens. This was one tough school.

Well, I spoke for an hour and forty-five minutes, and a hundred teens stayed after to be counseled. During that time, these outwardly tough teens cried out their pains and learned to say no to going along with the crowd. I still receive letters from some of those students who are not only turning from the pressure to do drugs, have premarital sex, and drink alcohol, but are learning to say yes to life.

From Cheryl I learned to have compassion and conviction. She is challenging teens to stand up for what is right, and to make their decisions based on what is in their hearts – not merely on someone else's challenge or dare.

The question is not, "Are you following someone?" It's "Who are you following?"

Leadership Check

Before following any leader, ask yourself the following questions:

1. Is this a person full of anger or bitterness?

Recently I met Anthony. One of the most important things in this man's life is education, and he has all the college degrees to prove it. Yet, despite all the learning, he is empty inside, and you can see it in his eyes.

Because Anthony's life is empty, he tries to fill the space in many different ways. One week he tries booze; another week he tries to pick up women. He spends so much time at work that he's become a workaholic. But his compulsion to fill his life in this manner has only made him lonelier. His marriage is nearly ruined, and he has no close friends.

When I talked to Anthony, I learned that his father had never allowed him to talk back, argue, discuss, or share his opinion on any subject. He had to go along with whatever this unloving father decreed. That meant following a long list of things to do -- and an even longer list of what not to do.

Anthony's background helped me understand why he always hated his bosses at every job. He'd had a father who did not seem to love him, and he'd rejected others who could help heal those hurts. I hope that some day Anthony comes to know and get along with his father, but right now his life is one of rebellion. If anyone lets this man be an influence in his life, he will probably regret it.

When you get to know your friends, if you see some real anger and bitterness, get them help if possible, but get out of the relationship before it blows up in your face.

2. Does this leader put others first?

Is he merely trying to please people, or is he considerate of others? This does not mean the person you admire should be a doormat – he shouldn't starve himself while he feeds the world, for example. But you should seek out a leader who takes pleasure in other people's accomplishments, and enjoys making others feel good.

The salesman who sells a million dollars of goods a year but never spends time with his family is not really a success. If a business owner grows his enterprise but treats his staff so badly that they all leave, he is also a failure.

Those who seek to be successful at the cost of others are not the kind of leader you'll want to follow. Find someone who puts others ahead of himself.

3. Does this leader get along with others?

Relationship skills are part of any leader's abilities. Does he treat others with respect? Can she laugh at herself? When talking with others, is this person gentle or abusive? Notice if the leader you want to follow has good listening skills. Do others like her? Effective leaders get along with others.

Be careful, though. Be sure you weigh this skill with the first two qualities I mentioned. Many bad leaders seem to have the ability to get along with others. They may have a charisma that attracts others for a short time. But instead of motivating people, they manipulate them. Ask yourself whether this leader gives his best to others -- or takes their best from them? Is she good at getting along with others -- or simply getting what she wants out of them?

4. Is this leader humble or arrogant?

Humility is one of the marks of a true leader. A confident leader will not swagger or strut, but will walk with an air of peace about him because he has nothing to prove to anyone else.

5. Does this leader try to do what's right or please people?

Whose approval is most important to him? Can she speak the truth boldly even if others don't agree? Will this person sit next to an unpopular student even if others in her grade scoff her? Will they have the confidence to ask a question even if some of the so-called leaders in the class have made asking questions seem childish and uncool? Will you do what needs to be done in a difficult situation even if it means an inconvenience to you or being ousted by the popular group?

Look carefully at your life and the lives of those you follow. Make sure they do what's right instead of simply finding ways to become popular.

115

6. Does he or she believe in strong morals?

Can he or she tell right from wrong? Real leaders believe in these things. You cannot convince me that most students in middle school and high school can fully think for themselves. They look at their friends before responding to a question to see what others are doing before making a move. Being an individual in your school who respects yourself first, then others, is one of the strongest issues of our day, and it will only be overcome by strong people like you, with wisdom, courage, and tact. Believe in leaders who know what to stand for and how to do it. Watch and follow them, and you can become like them.

Never follow a leader who has trouble distinguishing right from wrong.

7. Can this person admit mistakes and faults and get help when it is needed?

Quality leaders admit their mistakes instead of hiding them.

Many teachers who want to be leaders are kept from being their best because they still carry their childhood pains. A teacher may have experienced a terrible childhood, or something bad may have happened to her, and she could carry that pain about, inflicting it on other people -- including her students.

Real leaders learn to forgive and ask forgiveness. They can say, "I'm sorry."

Those powerful words have meant a lot in my life. I've noticed that my kids learn more about the truth, the right thing to do in a difficult situation, and my life when I admit my mistakes.

A couple years ago I needed professional counseling to overcome the messages I received in the dysfunctional home in which I grew up. That willingness to get help saved my life -- and has made me a much better father and friend to my family.

8. Does this leader exhibit a forgiving spirit?

A few years ago, a friend of mine lost her policeman-husband in a traffic accident, while he was working on an accident scene. A teenage boy who was watching the aftermath of the initial accident, not the road, hit and killed her husband.

My friends had their best years ahead of them. They had just begun to travel. Success had just found them.

At the funeral, several of this woman's children wanted to see the teen who had killed their dad. She would not permit them to meet the boy, but moments after the funeral, she had her son drive her to the boy's house. She walked in and introduced herself.

What she found was a devastated teenager, as well as parents who felt his pain. She knew he would always remember this tragedy, and that he might carry burden of it with him for the rest of his life. Because she didn't want that, my friend told the boy that what had happened was an accident. "I don't want you to carry this pain with you for the rest of your life. So I fully and freely forgive you. Get on with your life," she advised. "Don't let this ruin you, because it was simply an accident."

That is radical love and forgiveness. That's the kind of example – the kind of leadership – I could follow without hesitation. She was living out her faith in the world, and her light shone brightly. Pain would linger, and time would be the greatest medicine, but she gave that teen the chance to heal within.

9. Can this leader clean up his life before cleaning up the world?

One of the first requirements for leaders is that they respect their family before trying to lead strangers. If there are students who are rude to others when they have nothing to add to their popularity, and then they treat you nice, you better realize that they are people users. You will be their next target once you stop benefiting them.

If a leader doesn't have control of his own life, you'd better not follow his advice for your life.

Choose your friends and leaders carefully, instead of believing all that you hear. I want you to get to know people by looking at their character, not just how good they look or how others perceive them. You can only do that if you take care in deciding who you should follow. Once you find those good leaders, hang around them enough and you will eventually become like them. Then carryover the good qualities you learn, and apply them to your own leadership. Use those skills when you lead, and pass them on to others.

Stand out for good!

Boldness and confidence are not the only elements that make up a leader, so before you follow someone, know what he or she stands for.

Checkpoints

1. Have you ever followed the wrong person? What happened? What did you learn from that experience?

2. Using the information on leadership you've read in this book, list some qualities that make bad leaders. (Hint: What are some of the opposites of the qualities you know you should build into your life?) Are you following some people like this? If not, what can you do about it?

3. Compare the attitudes of integrity-filled leaders to false leaders. Is there a big difference between the two? What is it?

4. List some integrity-filled leaders:

5. List some false or selfish leaders:

6. How many of the leadership qualities mentioned in this chapter can you see in yourself (even just a little)? How can you help them grow in your life? What kind of people do you need to follow so that this will happen?

15

The Other Side
of Leadership

"If your actions inspire others to dream more, learn more, and do more and become more, you are a leader".

– John Quincy Adams

We've spent a lot of time looking at you -- who you are and the qualities that will make you a good leader. But there is more to leadership than you. No one can lead without considering the part others play. You'll need to know how to get along with others, and how to evaluate the impact they have on your life.

Because others influence us every day -- and we influence them in return -- in the next chapters we'll take a look at the other side of leadership: the people around you.

See Others as They Are

It has already been discussed how, as a true leader, you must learn to view yourself accurately. Yet, if you want to lead effectively, you must learn to see other people accurately as well. Everyone has good points and bad points, but sometimes we only see one side of a person. And sometimes we make the mistake of measuring ourselves by others -- what they do or what they think of us.

Such comparisons can kill your self-esteem in a moment. In fact, comparison is the number one cause of inferiority. It can kill even the best vision you have for yourself.

How does that work? Easy. When you see another teen who looks perfect, do you ask if she has problems -- just like you? She may appear to have it all now, but do you consider that she may be making choices that could cost her tomorrow? Probably not. Someone else's life may seem perfect in comparison to your own, but are you really seeing the whole picture?

Nearly everyone in my high school admired Chuck and looked up to him. All Chuck had to do was change his hairstyle, and the male half of the school followed along. He was a great athlete, and he had lots of friends and plenty of dates. Everything seemed to be going great for him, and I sure envied him.

While Chuck partied, though, he became addicted to alcohol – and ended up an alcoholic. He had to marry his first wife while he was still in high school, and that responsibility killed his plans for a professional sports career.

Today, none of my old high school friends know what happened to Chuck; and I'm not sure how many times he's been married. No one from the old crowd admires Chuck's life today.

We all looked on the outside and thought Chuck had it made, but we were wrong. That's because we couldn't see the whole picture. We should have been looking for some inside qualities like:

- Honesty
- Integrity
- Self-discipline
- A willingness to serve others
- An ability to help others become successful
- Pride in the school
- Love for others (not just dates)
- Respect for parents
- A sense of community responsibility

Those things were missing from Chuck's life. We did not see him as he really was because our vision had become clouded by his popularity.

Sometimes you will ignore a popular person's faults or limitations. At other times you may ignore a person's good points because you don't like his "package" – the way he looks. Either response can cause you not to see what is really there. Someone else's life may seem perfect in comparison to your own, but are you seeing the whole picture?

Can You See What Others Could Be or Do?

When you look at others, do you have the ability to envision the potential for greatness in them? To find out, answer these questions:

Can I see goodness in my family, friends, and acquaintances?

Can I recognize greatness in my friends?

Can I acknowledge others' abilities and suggest how they can use them?

Can I envision worthwhile goals that will help others tap their potential?

Did you answer yes to all four questions? If so, you already have a vision for leading others. Do your best to build on that.

If you only answered yes to three, identify where you need to build your leadership skills. Right now make out a plan that can help you. Your plan might look like this:

Step 1:   Pick a few friends and observe them.

Step 2:   Notice a positive quality they possess.

Step 3:   Tell them that you notice this quality, and encourage them to use it more in school, sports, social occasions, or at home.

Step 4:   Ask your friends what you can do to help them reach their goals.

If you can follow these steps, you will be on your way to habitually bringing the best out in others. Leaders make other people feel good and look good. Go and give it a try!

If you only said yes to one or two of the above questions, make a conscious decision to think of others and learn to encourage them. Look at some people who could become your role models. Learn from them how to lead.

Encouragement Exercise

If you need to build your ability to recognize greatness in others, start with your family. Can you appreciate the talents of your brothers and sisters? Maybe your older brother is good in sports, your sister is talented in writing, and your younger brother is handy with mechanical things. What can you do to help them achieve in these areas? Start to help and encourage them to do their best with their particular talent(s).

Now practice sizing up other people in the same way. When you practice seeing the best in others, you'll increase your vision for them.

Every person has been given skills to develop and use for the benefit of others. Help your friends discover what gifts they have been given, and encourage them to use those abilities to achieve their goals. Challenge your friends to fulfill their best dreams.

Look through the eyes of others, feel through their hearts, and help make this world more than it was when you came into it. Perhaps you will challenge your friends to stand out and do their best. On days when they have trouble seeing their own goals, renew their vision. By helping them to keep hoping during times when hope seems lost, you will pass on to them a point of view that most people lack.

Giving Up or Holding On

When is it time to give up on people? I met a principal whose answer to that was "never". One of his teachers once became exasperated with a student who always made trouble in her class; but the principal recognized that the troublemaker was acting in a loud, disruptive way, always bringing attention to himself, because of the pain in his home. This boy was a fulltime discipline problem, which made both teacher and class miserable.

One day the teacher went to the principal and asked him to remove the boy from her class.

"I can remove him, if you don't mind giving up on him," he answered.

"I don't want to give up on him. I just want him out so I can have a better class," she explained.

"We can get him out of there. If you think we should give up on him, then we will kick him out immediately."

"It's not that I want to give up on him. I just can't teach with him there!" exclaimed the frustrated teacher.

"The moment you want to give up on him, let me know, and I will have him put someplace else."

Finally she understood and replied, "I will never give up on him."

Most of us would like to have someone who will never give up on us, who will always keep holding on; and if we would look around, there is usually someone who is pulling for us and trying their best to encourage us to become our best and not settle for less. Pass on that hope. Is there a friend or classmate you've been tempted to give up on? What can you do today to offer a little strength, hope, and determination to that person?

You may even be able to find ways to encourage people you don't even know personally. Mr. Fitzwilliam, a farmer in North Dakota, had a vision for youth. Though he had a gigantic farm to tend to, he worked hard to bring in speakers who could present humorous, yet life-changing, messages to the kids in his area. He spends some of his spare time now as chairman of a group that schedules speakers on a regular basis. He does not know every teen at the rallies he arranges, but he is making a difference in their lives nevertheless.

Look for Ways to Bring Out the Best in Others

Can you be the catalyst that makes someone see things in a fresh way? Can you challenge those about you to brainstorm ideas and come up with possibilities that could help solve a problem, improve someone's life, or keep someone from hurting themselves or someone else?

Perhaps today you will encourage a faltering student to keep on studying, and someday she will discover the cure for cancer. Maybe you will challenge your brother to

125

reach out to the world and end hunger or discrimination, and he will go on to change society. Your vision for loving and complimenting could help someone become so much more.

Tips for Complimenting Others

1. Be sincere. Don't say it if it's only flattery.
2. Use their name. People love to hear their names spoken.
3. Make eye contact. Don't look elsewhere when complimenting someone. It suggests you have something to hide.
4. Be specific. Say "I like the way you respect your mom," instead of "I like the way you get along with people." The second statement is too vague.
5. Be brief. Compliments shouldn't go on and on. You'll only make the other person feel uncomfortable.

Rich Mullins, the Christian music artist, went back to school so he could get his degree and teach at-risk kids on an Indian reservation. He also took two days out of his busy schedule to talk and sing and offer encouragement to a fan he'd never met before. I was that fan. His compassion is affecting the lives of others. You, too, can encourage creativity and touch the lives of others.

Tips for Helping Others Be More Creative

1. Encourage others to dream. Ask "What if...?" What if you could do anything for a living? What would it be?
2. Build others up. Everyone does better when others help us feel good about ourselves. Be an encourager.
3. No wrong ideas allowed. Creativity is like brainstorming. If you think it, say it. Be positive. Be daring.
4. Make a list of creative ideas. Write them down. This makes them personal and adds power to them.
5. Create a plan to make one of these ideas a reality. Get help from someone who is a positive thinking, strong-willed, risk taker. They will give you the encouragement you need. Go for it!

Challenge your friends to fulfill their best dreams.

Checkpoints

1. Do you often compare yourself to others negatively? Describe how that feels and why you do it. Are you seeing others clearly when you do it? How are you seeing yourself?

2. How do you see other people? Can you encourage them toward their goals? Can you help them learn what they can become? Can you challenge them to do better tomorrow than they have done today? Think of someone you have encouraged recently. What did you do? How did it influence that person?

3. Have you practiced giving someone a sincere compliment? If not, review the steps and make someone's day.

4. What can you do to be more creative yourself? Who did you help develop their creative powers? Take a risk, step out of your comfort zone, and make the world a better place.

5. How do right and wrong influence your goals? Review your goals carefully. Do you need to reevaluate any of your planning to avoid doing wrong?

16

How Can I Help Others?

"Don't walk in front of me, I may not follow; Don't walk behind me, I may not lead; Walk beside me, and just be my friend."
– Albert Comus

You talk about being a leader, not a follower; but how do you know if you are a leader?

Leaders have the following characteristics:

- They contribute to their classes, families, and schools. They are always part of helping, not hurting.
- Instead of tearing down others, they build them up. While others start fights, they settle differences.
- They are in control of themselves.
- They care for others.
- They walk their talk.
- They are not bossy, so people can look to them for creative solutions to their problems.
- They know right from wrong.
- They ask questions without fearing those who might call them dumb.
- They stand up for the less fortunate.
- They have great compassion for the hurting.
- They usually believe in causes more than their own enjoyment.

How many of these qualities do you have?

I'd like to tell you about one leader. A couple of years ago, Josh McDowell, who has spoken to more college and high school students than anyone else alive, invited about 100 speakers to be part of his "Why Wait?" weekend retreat, in California. He taught us creative ways to show teens why they should wait until marriage to have sex.

We all arrived at the retreat site within the same twenty-hour period. Guess who carried most of our bags to our rooms? Not the bellboy, but the man who had a million things on his mind that would make the conference a success: Josh McDowell.

Now that's leadership!

Being a leader means being willing to help and serve others. If a person has too much self-importance to serve others, he or she is no leader. That means you do dishes and clean your room before you clean up your town. It means you look for other students in the halls and classes who could use either a smile or an uplifting or encouraging word, or you invite a student who is struggling to sit with your group at a game.

Leadership means helping your dad wash his car. How is this demonstrated with your little brother? Maybe you do it by being nice, or at least, not trying to get even. Though being nice to your brother may seem like a radical thought, I think it's part of an overall attitude that will get you the farthest in life.

I know someone who is hurting, but he won't tell me what the problem is. How can I help him open up?

You cannot force anyone to share with you, but you can open the door, gently and quietly. Begin by following these guidelines:

1. Develop an icebreaker. When a professional counselor first sees a family, he may have a parent share all the problems she has with the child. After Mom lists the sixty-nine things John has done wrong, the counselor turns to the child and says, "I bet you're delighted to be here today, aren't you? You probably couldn't wait to get out of school and rush in here with your mom, so

she could tell me about these things you do to upset the family life."

2. If that doesn't raise a chuckle or let the child know the counselor is open to his side, he might add, "It's tough raising parents today, isn't it?"

3. When you counsel with a person, you, too, need to let him know things are not one-sided. Build up some hope. Perhaps you can have the teen answer the question, "What things would your mom or dad say are wrong with you?" After the teen lists five or six things, bring in creative humor to show him there is some hope. Get him to laugh and realize the moment will pass.

4. Ask him to define the problem as he sees it. More than likely this will be very different from mom or dad's point of view.

5. Encourage him to seek possible solutions to the problem. Ask what he has tried in the past. Make a list of things that have and haven't worked. The more clearly the person you counsel sees his problem on paper, the easier he will find it to understand. In addition he will be able to see that he can get through this.

6. Offer additional counseling. You may discover that another counselor could better help this person. Maybe you know someone who has lived through a similar problem and has discovered steps that work. Don't be afraid to refer him if you know more help is available.

I know I need help, but I just can't seem to tell anyone. How can I develop the courage to ask others for it?

No matter what problem you have, sooner or later you will have to deal with it. You can wait, and the problem may get worse, or you can tackle it now, while it's smaller.

By admitting that you have a problem, you have already shown wisdom. Now you need to take action. Begin by focusing on the fact that talking about your problem will get it out in the open, where you can deal with it. Don't put your eyes on the difficulty of speaking, but on the benefits that may result from sharing your trouble. Find solutions, people, ideas, encouragement, and hope. You don't have to live in the middle of something that's too big to deal with alone. Learn to live free from worries. Get help!

I'm concerned about someone. I know he is hurting, but how can I approach him so he won't take it the wrong way? He hasn't let me help before, but things seem to be getting worse.

The fact that you want to help your friend shows you have feelings of empathy and a desire to help. Those are all good. They will help you as you try to give this friend a hand.

Here are some other things to remember:

1. *Chances are that your friend is crying out for help.* He just doesn't know how to express his need. Put yourself in his place. What has it been like to hurt in your own life? How have others helped you? You seem willing to help him now.

2. *You may be the only person who can feel his hidden pain.* Don't let fear keep you from becoming part of the solution. Later he may thank you for taking that first step.

3. *You could wait too long.* Don't let his story be part of the daily news; then it will be too late. He shouldn't have to slit his wrists before anyone has the courage to offer help. Go to him. If you feel uncomfortable doing it alone, find someone who can help you, and go together.

I know what it's like to be in that kind of situation. Several years ago I waited too long to help a friend who I knew was hurting. He hung himself, and to this day I regret not acting on the intuition that told me to help him.

You can't help someone who will not let you. If he still remains closed up, you cannot push him. But leave him with the message that he can turn to you if he changes his mind.

If the situation seems impossible, keep these guidelines in mind:

1. *If he will not share with you, leave him with hope.* Share the truth that there is an answer to every problem. Give him some reason to believe that life can become better.

2. *You may need to share the need.* If you have reason to believe this is a life-threatening or extremely harmful situation, go to an adult and tell what you know. Don't carry too heavy a burden on your own shoulders. Do not spread the news around among your friends. You are not a trained counselor -- get help.

A girl came to me for help, but her problem is too big for me to handle. What should I do? Should I tell her to come back later, or send her to someone else?

When someone comes to you with a problem that you cannot provide counsel for, don't simply tell her to come back, unless by doing so, you will be able to provide the help she needs. Instead, stick with her until you can connect her with others who can provide assistance.

Even if you can't solve all her problems, you can still help her by:

1. *Listening.* Show her that you care enough to be there when she needs you -- to listen without interruption, to concentrate on and understand what she says. Listen to her the way you would like someone to listen to you when you have a problem. Don't jump in with possible solutions before she has finished telling the whole story. Listening means "open ears, close mouth".

2. *Admitting your limitations.* If you can't provide adequate counsel, don't fear admitting it to either yourself or to the person in need. Let her know, though, that you can put her in touch with someone who will help her.

3. *Contacting another counselor.* Take her to an older, wiser person: a school counselor, a caring teacher, or someone trained to find an answer.

By taking these steps, you will let her know her situation is not hopeless. Together with caring counselors, you can find an answer.

How can I convince people I will keep their stories and problems confidential if they share them with me?

Are you a peer listener or just a friend who wants to help others? If you are a friend, follow these guidelines:

1. *Don't be a blabbermouth.* If you spread a person's troubles allover school, no one will want to share with you. After all, you wouldn't want an embarrassing story about you to become public knowledge. How much less a person with a serious problem wants it known.

2. *Earn the trust of others.* Even if you don't have a reputation for talking about others' problems, you need to let them know you will be openhearted and trustworthy. Until your friends know you won't broadcast anything and that you will not be overly judgmental, they will not feel secure.

3. *Know when you've reached your limits.* As a friend, you can offer an ear. Listen carefully and support the other person, but do not provide advice when the situation has gone beyond a friend's control. Instead, refer your friend to a trained counselor who can provide in-depth help. By listening, you have done right, but remember you cannot solve everything alone.

If you are a peer listener, the above truths are for you, but so are a few more:

1. *Understand your school's policy.* Know what you can and cannot do. Adults should have set the rules, and counselors and trained professionals should provide advice. Abide by their guidelines.

2. Keep things confidential. The confidentiality rule is twice as important for a peer counselor. Only discuss a person's problems with your adult advisor and possibly another peer counselor, if he or she needs to know something. Never share such problems with your friends. Even the juiciest story should remain in confidence. Remember, your talking could have serious consequences for the person who shared the problem.

3. *Know when to break confidentiality.* Whenever you counsel someone, begin with this rule: I will keep everything confidential, unless doing so means you or someone else would be at risk in the situation -- in danger of abuse or suicide. If you must break confidentiality, tell only a trusted counselor who can help the situation.

If you become trustworthy, people will open up to you. Strive to keep these effective counseling rules.

I want to become a peer listener and help other teens. How can I convince the rest of the school -- even just a few kids -- that I can help?

Is there a peer counseling program in your school? If so, join it; if not, you may want to help start one. However, you will need the cooperation of your school in order to do it there. Establish a good relationship with the administration, teachers, and the proper professionals. Their backup becomes essential if you run into problems you cannot handle. Do not seek to do it with students alone.

1. *Begin by getting the proper training.* Once you have done this, let other students know you are a peer listener and have been trained to listen and initiate help.

135

2. *When you start, gain small successes.* Help those with small problems first, to gain some experience. Don't immediately take on the largest problem in your school, because failure at that may stop you in your tracks.

3. *Ask the school what problems they most need help with.*

Form a committee of adults and students; then put out a survey to find out where the student body needs you most. Let your school know you are for real and that there is hope. You can be part of the solution to the hopelessness among your peers.

Forming a peer-counseling network or becoming part of an established counseling team may not be easy, but stick with it. You'll want to convince students that you have an answer they may not have found elsewhere. Above all, remember you are a listener, not a trained counselor.

17 Mean-What-You-Say Communication

"If you tell the truth you don't have to remember anything."
– Mark Twain

A little while ago, I almost lost a long-term friendship because my friend and I both thought we had a one-way relationship. Except, while I felt I was the one who always had to call him, he felt he actually initiated things more. We seemed caught in a trap.

I felt embarrassed to admit that I needed my friend and that his friendship was important to me, but I'm so glad I did. When I told him, he agreed with me. "I need it, too," he said, "but ...." He then began to detail past troubles that he'd never admitted bothered him. All this time he had hidden the anger he felt.

"Hold on, I have hurts, too," I said, and as I told him my side, he expressed surprise that I too had held the pain so deep inside.

Our long friendship – one that had brought our families together for numerous fun times – almost ended because the two of us had not communicated clearly about how we felt. We saved that friendship by crying and talking and becoming honest with each other. Most of all, we shared our words and feelings; we communicated.

To have good friendships, healthy families, and a positive social life, we need to be able to communicate clearly and deeply. Let's look at some practical tips for relating well to people at home, at school, and in our communities.

Let's Talk About Talk

Talk ... that's what communication is really about, isn't it?

137

No!

Listening is the greatest communication skill you can learn. To really hear another, you must understand what a person says, feels, and means. It requires that you temporarily put aside your own ideas, accept that person as being important, and give of yourself. If you don't do these things, you might be hearing, but you have not listened.

When you talk to a friend, teacher, or parent, who is more important: you or that other person?

Do you fight to get in your next sentence, or do you tune in to what's going into your ears?

Do you take that person's words to heart, or are you too busy thinking about either how you plan to respond or what she will think about your next sentence?

Here is some attitude advice for people who want to communicate clearly: "Don't be selfish; don't live to make a good impression on others. Be humble, thinking of others as better than yourself." I am not advising you to lay down and role over if someone is using or abusing you. We are talking about talking and listening, and if you want to be a good communicator it is vital that you learn to put others' needs before yours when they are talking.

True listening requires that you put that person first for a while and treat him with true respect.

Well, no one else does that for me, you may be thinking. Don't copy the behavior and customs of others unless they are wise and have the people skills that you want to practice in your own life.

You don't have to respond in the same way that students who are full of themselves do by implying to people they are not important enough to get a hearing. Putting yourself on a communication pedestal that way shows you feel that only your own words have importance.

Start to listen to others, and you will often discover that they begin to spend more time asking about your concerns. Address their deepest concerns, and they are more likely to hear yours.

Talk That Listens

Does communicating well mean you never open your mouth? Of course not; but it does mean that when you speak you do so wisely, following this advice:

1. Don't use bad language. Say only what is good and helpful to those you are talking to. Make your words a blessing to others.

    Have you noticed how popular the put-down is? Can you get through a day without hearing one? It's easy to find fault with others, but it's not wise, and it will only put you on the lower level -- not the one headed for the high road of leadership and mentorship.

    Instead, only say the things about another that you would say in front of people you admire. This rule eliminates the "Guess what I heard about So-and-So" type of conversation, and replaces it with something better.

2. Edify others. To edify someone means you build him up, instead of tearing him down. Before you unload on your friend, consider what it will mean to her. Will it ruin her day for no good reason? Will it help her with a problem she faces?

Do you lift up others or wipe them out with your words? Do you have good conversational habits, or do you need to develop new ones? Take the Communication Quiz to find out.

Communication Quiz

Check off the following traits that are part of your communication.

___ I share my feelings with others.
___ I talk openly and honestly with people.
___ In general, I try to trust people and look for the best in them.

___ When others talk, I look directly in their eyes and really tune in to what they say.

___ If I don't understand what someone means, I politely ask questions.

___ I'm aware of nonverbal communication in others. (If they look angry, fold their arms, seem bored, or act depressed.)

___ I try to be sensitive to others' feelings.

___ I always take into account the speaker's background and age.

___ I look carefully at the facts when I communicate.

___ I'm positive by nature.

___ If someone smiles or laughs at what I say, I feel good inside.

___ I pull for others on a regular basis.

___ Being a supportive friend is important to me.

___ If others disagree with my ideas, I try to learn from their point of view.

Did you check most of these? If so, you are an effective communicator. Did you find some places to improve on? Then know that you can learn better communication techniques.

Now review the following traits, and again check off those that are part of your communication.

___ I hold my feelings inside. I figure that close friends should just know how I feel.

___ I'm quiet, and it's hard for me to share with others.

___ I have trouble trusting people. There are a lot of creeps out there.

___ I try to do most of the talking when I communicate with others.

___ It's easy for me to forget people's names, even moments after we've met.

___ When I talk with others, I look around the room from time to time to see who else is there.

___ If someone is hurting inside, I figure it's her problem. Besides, what could I do anyway?

___ It's easy for me to be negative and pessimistic.

___ If someone smiles as I walk by, I think he is laughing at me.

___ I've got too many problems of my own to worry about helping others.

___ I wonder why people don't like me or wait on me more than they do.

___ I easily get angry if others disagree with me.

If you checked most of these, you have some poor communication habits.

Did you see a pattern to your problems? Perhaps you:

- Are too busy thinking about yourself to communicate well
- Think negatively about others and want to avoid them
- Fear people, because they might harm you
- Don't want to become involved with people

Much of your happiness in life will depend on how well you interact with others. If you fear people, ignore them, or can't be bothered with them, you have formed some poor habits that may harm you for life. Relationships with friends, your spouse, and employers will deeply depend on your skill in hearing what they mean and in telling them your own thoughts. So begin to practice caring for others today.

Communication Obstacles

Communication is a learned skill that you can work on. After you have talked to someone, you might need to review what transpired. Did you make some of the communication mistakes listed above, or did you demonstrate positive communication methods? Maybe you were blocked by some of the following common communication obstacles:

1. Disagreement between words and actions. Your behavior is a form of communication in that it communicates something about you. Do your words and actions agree, or do you say one thing and do another?

From the letters I've received about date rapes, I know that sometimes they happen when words are not consistent with actions. For example, when a couple has been drinking and dancing for hours, and they end up in his place at 3:00 A.M., trouble is often waiting to happen. A woman who willingly lies naked on a bed and then says, "no", has little credibility.

I'm definitely not suggesting that a man ever has an excuse for rape, but when words and actions disagree, the stage is set for something to go wrong.

To communicate clearly, check that you are not giving a hidden message. Your mind might be going in one direction, and your emotions in another; that will cause confusion for the listener. It can cause problems even in a situation much less devastating than a date rape. Make every effort to think and speak clearly, and to act in a manner consistent with what you say.

2. Too much noise. If you are talking to your friend while the music is blasting, he might not hear or understand. Don't ask your parents a question when they are deeply involved in an intense movie. Outside noise like this does not aid good communication.

You also have inside noise generated from the hurts, thoughts, and preoccupations in your mind and heart. While you feel distracted by them, you do not communicate well. Leave your inside noise at home for a time while you listen. If you suspect that inside noise interferes from the other person's side, discover what it is, so that clear communication can begin.

3. Too much or too little space. Did you know that how well you hear may be influenced by how close a person stands to you? People have natural assumptions that go with distance.

142

For example, if a person you've just met stands in your face, you probably try to back away. You don't know him well enough to feel comfortable that close up. If your dad yells, "I love you," from across the room, when you're really hurting, it won't have the same impact as if he stands next to you and puts an arm around your shoulders and says the same words. How close or near you are to people communicates its own message.

Here's a rule of thumb about distance for most Americans (other nationalities may differ):

Public distance: Stay 10 - 14 feet from a public audience.

Social distance: Stay 4 - 6 feet from others at a business meeting.

Personal distance: A distance of 1 - 2 1/2 feet is appropriate when you talk to casual acquaintances.

Intimate distance: Intimate distances extend out to 18 inches from close friends and family.

4. Inconsistent tone of voice. Has anyone ever yelled this at you: "I said I wasn't mad, didn't I?" Did you believe what she said? In this case, her tone said much more than her words. Or maybe someone told you, "Okay, I forgive you. Now I don't want to hear any more about it," in a hurt tone of voice. You didn't believe his hurt was over and that he'd forgiven you, did you?

When you say things you don't mean, your tone of voice may give you away. Watch what you really mean, and say it in a tone of voice that backs it up, or don't say it at all. Become aware of what people really mean when they act this way, and talk things out if you think they are not saying what's really in their hearts.

5. Slang that confuses. Mary and Judy had a confusing conversation:

Mary: "Sue's parents are strange."

Judy: "You mean they're weird."

Mary: "No, just strange. They really act weird sometimes, but not weird-weird – if you know what I mean."

Judy: "I'm sorry, I dont know what you mean. Do you like them?"

Mary: "What do you think? They act like kids. I went to their house, and the dad, well, he is so hyper, and he was telling the strangest jokes I've ever heard. And the mom acts like a sixteen-year-old."

Judy: "Boy, I'm never going there."

Mary: "Why not? They're neat parents. My mom's a lawyer. She's so stuffy and boring. Not Sue's parents. They come to all her games and work with the church youth group. I wish mine cared as much about what I do and acted so good with my friends."

Judy: "Boy, this talk sure was strange. I'm glad you say what you mean and mean what you say -- you know what I mean?"

Judy felt glad when that conversation ended (and so did I). Mary took the word strange and gave it her own definition, and she seemed to be inconsistent with her ideas. If she's always so confusing to talk to, can you see why others might either avoid her or simply call her -- you guessed it! -- strange?

The same goes with the slang you hear in school. Does your mom know what "bad" means in your world, or will you confuse her when you use the word? Clear communication requires that each person understands the definition of a word, and that ideas be presented clearly.

Miscommunication causes trouble in school, sports teams, marriages, business situations, and churches. When you don't know what others think, how they feel, or why they made a critical decision, you cannot clearly identify problems and their solutions.

Good communication opens people up, allows them to grow closer, and lets them feel good about themselves. Spend time discovering your own communication style. Develop clearer ways of speaking and writing. You'll see changes in your life and in your self-esteem.

18 Friends, Cliques, & Other Serious Problems

"The only way to have a friend is to be one."
– Ralph Waldo Emerson

I talk with a lot of students before, during, and after my visits to schools. I also leave my address at places where I speak, and get the opportunity to answer thousands of letters. Since you are a leader, you should know what other teens are asking, as well as some possible answers to these very important questions. You may even feel like asking a question yourself. Ask me in person if I ever come to your school, and if that isn't a possibility, feel free to write me. Understand, these are just my answers; you may have some better ones. If so, please send them to me so I can offer them to those in need.

You talk a lot about making your brother or sister a friend. How can I do that?

It's a good idea to make your brother or sister a friend, because that relationship could benefit you both for your whole lives. By getting started now, you can enjoy closeness for many years. To help you with that goal, follow these steps:

1. *Look at things from your brother's or sister's point of view.* Your younger brother may just want to be part of your group. Your older sister may be feeling the pressures of looking for a college or finding a job. When you relate to them, take into account how each person thinks and what it's like to be that age.

2. *Be considerate of your brother or sister.* To make this step easier, think about what it would be like to be an only child. If you think it would be fun, ask an only

child about the loneliness. Talk to a friend who has no brothers or sisters, to see it from another perspective. Perhaps you've taken your family for granted.

3. *Don't let others keep you from this friendship.* How much does peer pressure affect how you treat your family? Most teens fight with a sibling -- at least some of the time -- because their friends do it. Just because your friend doesn't think it's cool to be pals with his brother, does that mean you can't turn your sister into a friend? Decide for yourself.

How would you feel if your brother or sister had been killed? Would you wish you'd done something differently? Make those changes before it's too late.

Why do special cliques have to exist in our school?

It hurts to feel left out. No one likes to feel as if she were "on the outside, looking in." No guy wants to feel he could never be part of the team or liked by the best-looking girls in the class. But believe it or not, there are some positive reasons why you have certain groups in your school:

1. *Part of it is normal, healthy, and necessary.* When people who share interests get together, they can form better friendships. If you hate baseball, you'd never feel comfortable on the baseball team. Likewise, people who can't stand chess don't really want to be in the chess club; and chances are, they don't have many friends on the chess team because of their different interests. It's the same way with other groups of people.

2. No one can have lots and lots of intimate friends. Building deep friendships takes time and effort. About the largest number of close friends you could have would be four, and at times you may only have one; but when you have four good friends, you may not be as close to any of them as you'll be to that one.

Though you can know lots of people, and care for them, you can't become truly close with twenty or thirty people at once. No one has the energy or time necessary to nurture so many deep relationships.

So limiting friendships is not all bad, if it causes better relationships based on common interests and goals.

Groups can become negative, however, when they have the wrong attitude about their limitedness.

No group should:

1. *Put down other people.* Not everyone shares the same interests. Just because others are not in the group is no reason to label them as bad.

2. *Look out for only their own benefit.* Such groups become self-destructive. Nothing lasts long when it has only its own good at heart.

3. *Ridicule others because of some "lack".* What makes any one group think that it is the best measure of people? No one has the right to gossip, be mean, or make fun of someone else who is less attractive or smart. No clique should make a person who is "different" suffer for the rest of his life.

People may want to be part of groups that do these things, but you can do better for yourself. Set yourself a higher standard.

How do you relate to groups in your school?

Ask yourself:

1. *Am I a member of a clique?* If so, how do the people in it influence you? How do you influence them? Are the morals they have good for you? I talk with many kids who became involved with drugs or partying because "the group was doing it." They didn't have the courage to stand up for themselves. Don't let yourself fall into that trap.

2. *Am I feeling left out?* Perhaps you feel as if you don't belong to the right group. Do you want to be friends with a certain clique mainly because of their status? If so, you could spend your life vainly searching for the "right" group. Instead of looking at externals, you need to find friends who show they are honest, sincere, have a sense of humor, and are easy to get along with.

3. *Do I reach out to new people?* Never assume you will not like someone new. She could end up being your next best friend or a lifelong pal. Give people a chance. If you were in her place you'd want a fair opportunity.

4. *Occasionally you will find someone who just never fits in.* No matter what you do, he may remain beyond your group, but at least offer him the opportunity to become a friend. Give a person a chance, or he may remain isolated and hurt.

5. *Am I avoiding the pettiness of some groups?* Compassion and kindness are lost arts in today's world. You may have received unkind treatment from other people, but that doesn't mean you have to join in their naughty reindeer games.

You may never change every group in your school, but you can start with yourself and encourage your friends to develop these attitudes. Everyone in the school will never be close to you, but you'll probably have some good friends.

Ever since my friend got mad at me for something I did, I have felt angry inside and not myself. Do you think there's a connection? What can I do about it?

There sure is a connection; fortunately, there's also a cure. Whenever I get mad at my wife or a good friend, something happens inside me: my desire to say, "I'm sorry; will you forgive me?" turns completely off, and I no longer feel like being nice to anyone. Instead, the natural thing to do is to get angry and think of getting even. At this point, I don't want to be around anyone.

That's the problem with inside hurts and pains: they close off our feel-good buttons. But if you right that wrong, then like magic, your feel-good button and desire to get closer to that person will both work again.

Let me encourage you to go to your friend and say, "I'm sorry I hurt you. Let's not let (whatever happened) break up our friendship. Please forgive me."

One of the best guidelines for friendship is, "Be a big enough person to go and make things right with your friend."

Understand, you can't carry a grudge against your friend and still have peace inside yourself. You get to choose which thoughts you carry with you and dwell on. Let others carry thoughts of anger, bitterness, and wanting to tell someone off. You are not average. You are a leader. Choose today to do what's right -- not what's easy. Remember, the kind of life you desire starts with you, and its starts today.

My best friend and I had a major fight. I apologized, but he still won't talk to me. It's been a long time. What can I do?

Trying to put a friendship back together can show your friend how important he is to you. But you may have to be patient before he sees that. Take the following steps:

1. *Begin by going to your friend.* Apologize for your part in the problem. If he does not accept the apology, it is no longer your problem – it's his. You cannot force him to be your friend, but you have tried to make peace between you.

2. *Keep your cool.* If you apologize and your friend gets angry, don't react in anger and get mad allover again. A good friendship allows for personality differences. Be a good friend.

3. *Be patient.* Once you have apologized, give your friend time to get over his anger. People recover from hurts at different rates. You may let things blow over easily, but your friend may hold onto anger for a while longer.

4. *Think about this friendship.* Ask yourself, "How important is this to me?" If you have to eat humble pie, then do it. Call your friend and be honest with him. Tell him you think this relationship is worth fighting for. People who risk nothing cannot have strong friendships. The closeness you gain can be worth the pain.

5. *Talk with your friend.* Ask him what he thinks caused the problem. Unless you get at the source, the problem will most likely come up again. Plan for it not to happen, and chances are it won't.

I have tried to be nice to an unpopular boy in my class, but even when I sit with him in the lunchroom – the way you suggested – he rejects all my efforts to be friendly. What now?

First, ask yourself, "Why am I being friendly to him?" Did you do it so other teens will admire you and pat you on the back? Do you want to be noticed? If so, he's sure to pick up on that. If you are not doing it for the recognition, but to help him, remember you need to keep on being tactful and pleasant. You may have to try to talk to this boy several times before he will talk back. Low self-esteem may keep him from speaking to you. At first he may find it hard to accept a compliment or almost never look you in the eyes, because he has been picked on, put down, and abused by others. Deep in the back of his mind, he wonders if you want something from him or if you are setting him up for some big heartache later. Much of this comes from a self-preservation instinct. Keep trying for a while, and you may gain some ground.

If he continues to refuse you, though, stop. You may have to settle for being nice when you see him in the hallway, or maybe you can tell him to call if he ever wants to talk. Make certain you never spread rumors about him. Stand up for him when he needs it. But at some point he has the right to be left alone, if he will not become friendly.

Give it a little more time if you've only made a few efforts to be nice. I think he will come around. Everyone needs someone like you, who is nice for the sake of being nice. Once you break down the wall, he may be happy to be friends.

My friend has a really serious problem, but she made me promise not to tell anyone about it. I want to tell someone, because I can't help her. How do I know if I should break confidentiality?

If your friend has a problem of incest or abuse, or if she is talking about suicide, you must break your promise. She needs help badly, but she will only get that help if you tell. Whenever someone is deeply at risk, when she could hurt herself or others, or when someone is hurting her, you need to find help. Remember, it is always better to have a live friend who can get mad at you than a dead, hurting, or abused friend, because you kept that problem a secret.

If at all possible, take your friend to someone in authority, to tell about the problem. If she will not go, go yourself.

When you counsel with someone, try not to promise ahead of time that you will not tell. However, if you make that promise without realizing what will be said, and the person you counsel tells you of one of the above problems, you must break the promise. You need to get help. It is said that in the long run, 100 percent of the time that person will thank you. Your friend cannot thank you if she does not live through her problem.

By breaking that trust, you do not betray her; you have been the most loyal friend she could have. You have acted in her best interests, because you truly want the best for her. You willingly placed your friendship on the line because you cared so much for her.

Recently one of my friends told me he was considering suicide, but then he laughed it off as if it were a big joke. Should I take him seriously?

Absolutely! Whenever someone implies suicide, talks about it directly, or tells you how, where, and why, take it seriously. Go to someone who can help: your parents, a concerned teacher, a counselor who cares about kids, your principal, or someone else.

Time after time I have heard that a suicide victim had told friends the details of his plan to take his own life. Those

151

friends either ignored him or responded, "You'll never do it," or, "That's a stupid thing, so don't think about it." In several situations, the person took his life just the way he said he would.

Don't ignore anyone who mentions suicide. If your friend says he will do it that night, do not leave him. Call for help. If he makes you promise not to tell anyone, it does not matter. In a life-or-death case like this, you must break confidentiality. Your friend will thank you in the end. Let him share, then get help immediately. You can handle your friend's angry feelings later.

I think the girl who has the locker next to mine is being abused at home. Should I do something, or should I mind my own business?

How often do we see newspaper reports of neighbors who thought the kid next door was being abused, but no one said a word because everyone felt it wasn't his or her business? By the time the tragedy turned deadly, it was too late to help the child.

Abuse **is** your business; it is everyone's business. Still, it is very important that if you sense something this serious, you go to an adult, not another teen. Do not start a rumor about your suspicions, in case you are wrong. Talk to your counselor, the principal, your parents, or a special teacher. Share the problem with that adult, and tell him or her why you suspect it.

Maybe your friend has given you some hints, implied that she was abused, or has simply come out and told you, making you promise not to tell. You must break that promise; while it may take a while, she will thank you in the end. Perhaps she will have to be taken out of her home, and the law may prosecute the adult who has done the abusing, but remember, you are the link to your friend's health, well-being, and possibly her life. You are her link to hope.

Often an abused teen drops hints because she wants someone to know. She may feel the abuse is her own fault, and she wouldn't know how to go to an adult herself. An abusive adult usually convinces the young person that she caused this to happen, that his actions are normal, that everyone does it, and that if the young person tells, she will regret it the rest of her life. But abuse is never caused by the frightened victim. **Never!**

Go seek help for your friend. If the first person won't listen to you, go to someone else. If need be, go to your abused friend and tell her what you have done. Explain that you have talked to an adult and you want her to, too. Or the adult you have confided in may talk directly to your friend. But whatever you do, get your friend the help she needs.

My friend just found out that she's pregnant, and she's considering an abortion. What can I tell her?

This is a crisis in which your friend needs a good friend to stand by her. How you respond may be a big help to her -- or a hindrance. Whatever happens, you must decide to remain her friend and help her find the counseling she needs.

1. *Begin by listening carefully.* Show your friendship by offering her two open ears and an open heart. Don't try to solve her problem before you have listened to her entire story. The time to advise is later.

2. *Once the initial shock has passed, help her realize the importance of making good decisions.* Many people will want to tell her what to do, and the confusion could overwhelm her. Stand by your friend to help her make a decision she need not regret for a lifetime.

3. *Encourage her to tell her family.* Naturally you will not want to do this if she comes from an abusive family that does not have her best interests at heart, but otherwise you need to encourage her to tell her mom and dad. She may fear that, but they need to have some input in this decision.

   Imagine if you were the mother, and your seventeen-year-old daughter had become pregnant. Wouldn't you want to help her choose? Wouldn't you want to be able to help her consider the options for adoption, or the option of allowing you to raise the child yourself?

153

4. *Get her to a good counselor.* There she can learn of the options.

   Those who encourage her to end the life of her child should tell her about post-abortion trauma. For the rest of her life she could wonder what that child could have been. Would he have been a scientist who discovered the cure for cancer? Could she have made great contributions to the world of art, or written a book that would help thousands? What would the child have looked like? The questions are endless. Help her avoid the guilt and pain of abortion by getting her to someone who will provide her with many positive opinions. The most convenient way out will not provide a simple solution to all her problems. Remind her that clinics that perform abortion seldom, if ever, let a woman hear the heartbeat of her unborn child inside her.

   It's also important that the counselor who encourages her to either have the child or give it up for adoption tells her of the pain of going through nine months of pregnancy and then letting go. There is also a lot of pain in wondering what the family is like who adopts her child. That's why she needs to learn of all of her options, and not make a hasty decision in the heat of the moment without being surrounded by those who love her and have her best interest at hand, as well as all the facts and options.

5. *Encourage her to consider adoption.* Compared to abortion, adoption is a loving option. Millions of loving couples who cannot have children would love to raise a baby in their fine homes. Why not give them the chance? She can read through their profiles and pick out the parents who would discipline as she would, as well as find out about the child being raised in a city or country and so on.

6. *Stick by your friend.* Don't abandon her, whatever happens. Show her you love by remaining her friend.

Remember, your friend will have to live with the decision for a lifetime. Help her make the right choice.

What do you have to say about so-called bad friends?

Here's a poem that I wrote when I recently broke my bonds with a friend who was leading me downhill.

Bad Friends

Some friends are good,
and some are bad.
I know because
of some I've had.
Friends are made for lots of fun,
but when it's over,
said and done,
was the fun good,
or was it bad?
Did it make you happy
or make you sad?
Think of last night.
Now are you glad ... ?
Do they like to cheat
or lie or steal?
When you hang with them
how do you feel?
Can you look yourself
in the eye,
or do you ask,
"Why did I
do this or that,
just for fun,
even though it hurt someone?"
Is sex their thing
or drugs or booze?
How do you feel
from what you choose?

If you regret
the things you do,
then that should be
your biggest clue
to break the bonds
of friends who lead
you into pride
or sin or greed.
And if they keep
on doing wrong,
it's time for you
to say, "So long."
And yes, you'll have
two tear-filled eyes.
But please don't ever
compromise.
For who you are
is what you'll be
now and through all
eternity.
Please be wise, don't compromise.
Be smart, don't start.
Use your head, don't end up dead.
If you must say no, do so.
'Cause you'll be happy in the end,
If you break the bonds of
bad friends.

What's wrong with going to parties where alcohol and other drugs are offered? After all, I always say no. Can't I just go to be with my friends?

You can go to be with your friends, but are you wise to? Look at the chances you are taking:

1. *You will gain the reputation of a drug abuser.* Merely being around these friends puts you in their crowd and labels you with their reputation: drug user and abuser.

2. *The crowd is stronger than you are.* I don't think anyone can go to such parties over an extended period of time and continually say no.

A man had a beautiful bird who knew over fifty songs. When he planned to go on vacation for two weeks, he took his priceless, unique bird to a friend, who raised common, everyday sparrows. He gave the friend careful directions on feeding and watering and everything else. His so-called friend said he'd follow the rules to the letter.

As soon as the songbird's owner left, the friend took the bird and placed him in the cage with his 100 common sparrows. He thought, *"My friend is gone, and he will never know, so I will put the songbird in with my sparrows, and in two weeks' time it will teach my sparrows how to say more than 'chirp, chirp, chirp'."*

When the man came back, took his bird home, and removed the cover from the songbird's cage, it could only imitate the sparrows' "chirp, chirp, chirp."

The crowd will bring you down. I have heard story after story of teens who have gone to such parties -- even going so far as bringing along their own soft drinks -- but in almost every case, those young people eventually ended up drinking and using drugs. Don't think you can hang around people who use drugs and not eventually take on their character qualities. If you won't, why do you have to stay around them? If you want to be popular with a group, it shows you really want their reputation.

3. *You could suffer the legal consequences.* If your friends get caught, you, too, could be arrested and prosecuted. Having charges filed against you merely because you were there is not worth it. Why take the chance of being guilty by association?

4. *You may have bad memories.* If someone at the party dies or another crime takes place (besides using drugs), you will have the memory of it for a long time. The pain is not worth it.

Be smart, don't even start going to such parties. Choose new friends who will not drag you down.

19 Leadership in the Balance

"Whether you think you can or whether you think you can't, you're right."
– Henry Ford

Would-be leaders may have many talents and gifts, yet unless they know how to handle their abilities, they may stand out not for their skills and qualities, but for other not-so-pleasant characteristics.

Leadership requires an often delicate balance. To help you strike that balance, I've identified some opposites you'll need to understand and keep under control.

Self-Confidence vs. Arrogance

When you walk with your head held high, believing you can face the future and have a healthy relationship with both your family and others, you have self-confidence. Instead of worrying about your past, you believe you are capable of making decisions -- and you can live with those decisions, right or wrong.

On those occasions when you are wrong, you can apologize, make amends (if possible), and move on. You can look people in the eye and offer them a sturdy handshake. Instead of worrying about looking foolish in front of others, you can aim at doing your best. Guilt or worries about others' opinions do not consume you.

However, you need to be aware that any skill you overuse can become a weakness. When you walk in confidence, unashamed of yourself, standing up for what is right, you remain strong. It's when you hold your head so high that your nose is in the clouds – when you won't recognize others around you, and when you become too "big" to help your parents with the housework and the lawn

159

– that you become arrogant and obnoxious. No one wants to stay around someone with that kind of pride problem.

Balance your confidence by developing a realistic opinion of yourself. If you use your own positive feelings about yourself to help others learn to appreciate themselves, you will be unlikely to step over that boundary. The truly humble person has the confidence and strength to be the leader he was meant to be. He can serve others without drawing attention to himself; he does that by opening a door for another, helping a friend with homework, or giving up the best seat at a play or game. Others will come first. When you can act as a servant to the people you see each day, you have true confidence.

Communicating vs. Being a Blabbermouth

Almost every leader I know is a good communicator. Real, effective leaders speak with confidence, and they speak the truth. Words are powerful tools -- more powerful than we sometimes believe. The next time someone says, "A picture is worth a thousand words," suggest that they read the Gettysburg Address, the Twenty-third Psalm, or Dr. Martin Luther King's 'I have a Dream' speech. Real communicators know that words influence people strongly.

But a good communicator also knows when the words have to stop. Overused, the skill of communication can become deadly. A good talker must know when to stop and listen.

Have you ever known someone who talked all the time -- you could never get a word in edgewise when you were with him? People don't stick around such folks for long, and they certainly won't follow their lead. Your goal is to have people glad when you come into a room – not when you leave.

Communication usually requires words, but it isn't limited to them. Have you ever told someone you loved her, with your arms folded and a steely look in your eyes? Did she believe you? Unless her back was toward you and she couldn't hear the bitterness and anger in your voice, it's doubtful that she did! In this case, your actions and tone of voice spoke louder than your words.

Or maybe you've been told, "I love you, but ...." Like most folks, you probably couldn't remember anything before the "but". Instead, your mind focused on the list of things the speaker felt mad about.

Do you need to improve your communication skills?

Find someone to help you learn and grow in this area. Go to a few good friends, your coach, an admired teacher, or your parents, and ask them to honestly answer your question, "Do I talk too much?" Then discover from them some ways you can become a better communicator.

Honest feedback from people who care for you can help shape your character – if you are willing to listen and act on good advice. It's like having a free counseling session, or inviting a consultant to enter your home and share ways in which you can become more effective. Companies pay thousands of dollars to have people provide such advice for them, and you can have it for free. But you'll need to ask, because most people will not simply offer you their opinions. Fear that you will get angry with them will deter all but a few people.

As you learn to communicate, you'll need to learn to shut your mouth sometimes. Make listening one of your skills, because you will need it often if you seek to reach out to others. Listen twice as much as you talk, and people will want to be around you. Remember, you have two ears, one mouth. Use them in that proportion. Encourage others to share their feelings and interests. Ask questions that make them feel good about themselves, and you will open the door to their lives. You will be learning how to win true friends and influence others.

Leadership requires an often delicate balance.

Making Good Eye Contact vs. Being "In Your Face"

Leaders look others in the eye, instead of peering around the room, seeking something better. When you sit down with a leader, she will pay attention to you, instead of waving at twenty others who pass by.

Focusing on your companion tells him he is important. I know I'm always impressed when people look at me instead of either avoiding my eyes or dividing attention between me and anything else around. People who won't make eye contact don't impress others with their concern. It's as if they have something to hide: kind of like when you did something wrong as a child (Or how about last week!) and totally avoided eye contact with your mom.

So make good eye contact with those you meet. Show them that you care, but don't get too close for comfort. An overconfident companion doesn't just look you in the face; he's in your face. You've experienced it when a stranger talks to you from six inches away. Perhaps you started backing away, or felt as if you'd like to bend over backwards to escape!

Most people feel comfortable with one-and-a-half to two feet between them and another person. Exceptions to this are a first-time meeting, or speaking with someone who is very shy. Such situations may require a little more space.

Don't let your newfound confidence irritate. Keep a balance in the distance you keep. Make a new friend feel comfortable by communicating, making eye contact, and staying just close enough to be friendly.

Serving Others vs. Neglecting Yourself

From the stories and ideas I've presented in this book, you've learned that leadership is synonymous with servanthood; it's not synonymous, however, with personal neglect.

Thinking of others, serving them, and meeting their needs, is something that great leaders who are admired and respected teach us to do. It's nearly impossible to remain depressed if you are helping someone else. At the same time, however, don't take yourself for granted or neglect your own real needs.

I've seen church leaders lose their families because they spent every night at church. Teachers and workaholics do the same with their loved ones. Others are so filled with false modesty and such a long guilt trip that they give all their efforts to others and leave nothing for themselves.

Don't believe that you are so unworthy of care that you must completely expend your energy on others. Instead, find a healthy balance in which you help others, but keep from draining all your energies.

Some leaders forget to keep themselves in shape emotionally. The hidden pains of the past may interfere with their ability to give to others, yet they seek to pour out all their emotional resources for the good of others. When they hurt, they need to reach for help themselves – perhaps even seek counseling.

You cannot lead well if you are out of shape mentally, emotionally, physically, or spiritually. So while you are helping a homeless woman by getting her a meal, helping your invalid neighbor by cleaning up his yard, visiting a friend in the hospital, or working with a youth ministry, remember to keep yourself in mind. Don't keep moving until you are exhausted; schedule in some rest time. You have legitimate needs, too. If you don't respect yourself, others will have a hard time with it as well.

Reading to Broaden Your Horizons vs. Hiding In Books

Leaders read in order to learn more about life, but they don't hide in a book. Again, striking a balance is so important.

Don't read only about one subject, or let your social life lapse because you feel compelled to read the latest novel. Overusing your skill and neglecting other areas of your life will keep you off balance.

When you are sitting (unless you are driving a car), go ahead and read. Listen to cassettes and CD's when you are on the move. Both will help you learn. But when a friend stops by, put down your book or turn off your CD player or MP3 player. Read when you are alone; listen to others when you have the chance.

I challenge parents never to read the paper while their kids are awake. If they are in the room with mom and dad, kids should receive the attention they need. Dads who hide behind the paper imply that the news is more important than their children. Moms who do the crossword puzzle during playtime give their youngsters the impression that they like the paper more than the kids.

Don't read at the expense of others. Make people a part of your life, and read in the quiet moments. The same goes with having earplugs in when you are with friends. Your music can wait. People are more important than things or your selfishness. When you are fortunate enough to have others around, take the time to focus on them and make them feel important.

Staying In Shape vs. Becoming a Fitness Freak

All of us need to stay in shape physically. If you need to get in shape, join a gym and work out. Get your heart rate to a good pace for your health, but don't become a pest about exercise and eating right. When your friends want to go out for junk food occasionally, don't spend the meal driving them crazy. Regularly harping on your diet will only make them want to avoid you.

Don't get addicted to exercise fads that will not last. Ask yourself how long you've been following your current regimen. If you have stuck with a good pattern for weeks or months, you will probably hang in there. If not, this may simply be a short-term fling with a new fitness program. So when you brag about it to your friends, you run the risk of making them feel bad about something that may be history in a short time.

Balance your need for exercise with the mental, emotional, and spiritual sides of your life. Physical things are important, but they are not the only thing in life.

Taking a Stand vs. Being Insensitive

When you lead others to avoid drugs, alcohol, tobacco, profanity, premarital sex, or other dangerous actions, don't be too hard on them. Though you can clearly see what's right and wrong, those you speak to may not have dealt with this area of their lives. Though they know right and wrong, they haven't personally acquired the same choice-making skills as you have. Deal gently with them, and you are more likely to affect their lives in a positive way.

For example, when you begin to believe the words and examples in this book, and start to act in a way that your parents and teachers and you are proud of, it might become second nature to you. As you gain an appreciation for doing things that are helpful and not hurtful or damaging to you or others, you alter your lifestyle. Then a fellow student comes along who hasn't had as much wisdom poured into them as you have. If you berate her for not knowing how to either communicate or have as good eye contact as you do, you are wrong.

When we act insensitively, it's often because we have become proud and arrogant. Putting down others because they don't know what we know means we have missed the point. Instead of recognizing that not all people have our knowledge and that we can learn from others, we have put ourselves on a pedestal.

When I train my children to work in the yard, fish, or paint a model car, I need to remember that this is brand new skill they are learning. If I act as if these skills should be second nature to them and scold them for either failing or doing poorly, I will discourage them. They have to start at the same level at which I started when I was a kid. It's the same in leadership matters. We are all children, and we grow at different rates in different places.

Though you know bad from good, don't become insensitive to others' feelings. Love them through the learning process.

Focusing on People vs. Focusing on Projects

Certainly every leader needs to have projects, and be able to stick to them. Whether it's the game you are playing this afternoon, studying for a test, exercising, or painting a room, you'll need to focus on the things you need to get done. But don't let projects push people out of your life.

You may need to work hard to accomplish your tasks, but when you please the boss with all the good you do for the company at the cost of seriously neglecting your family, you have obviously gone too far. People are more important than projects. Don't ever put projects ahead of a person.

For example, I am on my church basketball team. When I play, I have to remember that I represent something larger than myself. If I get angry at the final point because the ref made a bad call, I show the world that having faith in my life means nothing. I'm no different from the people who don't have faith. I never want winning to become more important than the message I give to others about how the game should be played and life should be lived.

Turning the Other Cheek vs. Knowing When to Fight

Turning the other cheek means that when someone is mean to you, instead of fighting back you take into account how they are possibly hurting inside. It means we repay meanness with kindness. When we are able to do this we become the bigger person, and have a great deal of power to affect lives in a positive and long-lasting way.

However, we are not to stay in the same place for years and let the same person smack our cheeks over and over. A wife should never stay in a home where she is being abused. At some point common sense tells us to leave such situations. The time may come when we need to stand for what is right.

A girl should look for traits in a boyfriend that indicate whether he has a temper and could abuse and use her. She needs to take immediate action by getting out of the relationship, and getting help if he is acting on his anger.

Knowing when to stand your ground and when to flee means we must choose our battles. What is worth standing up for? What is worth walking away from? When do you tell a friend you disagree with him, and when do you hold that thought inside?

Sometimes the answers are hard to come by. In such cases, you will want to consult a wiser person. If you feel angry about something your friend said, don't act at all. Wait until you cool down. Write down what you want to say, and hold on to it for six days. At the end of that time, if you still feel the same way, rip up the paper and go and tell your friend. Don't leave it on paper, but speak from the heart.

Balancing Act

If you want to lead, you'll need to balance these and other areas of your life. Identify areas in which you overreact or become overcommitted, and you will see the places where you need to make corrections. For example, it's great to save money for your future, but if money has become your god, you are out of balance. By looking at the attitudes that knocked you out of balance, and discovering ways to change them, you can change your life for the better.

Balance is an important component to leadership because it shows people our lives are not one-sided, that they are under control, and that they take the most important things into account. People who are out of control cannot expect others to look up to them or want to have lifestyles like theirs. Who wants to be out of control and suffer the pain that kind of life brings?

Along the way, don't forget to take care of your family and yourself. When your life becomes one of integrity and honesty, you will want to serve others because you will be filled with gratitude for all of the good things you appreciate.

A life with that kind of order to it will result in a happy, content person. A person like that can become a great leader because others will want to experience such joy – joy you live by each day!

Checkpoints

1. Have you known someone who had many gifts, but became obnoxious? Why did that person offend you?

2. List the areas in which leaders need to develop balance. Have you struggled with any of these? Why? What have you done about it?

3. Do you need to gain balance in some areas you've never really thought about? List a few, along with ideas about how you can get balanced. (If you need help, ask a friend, youth counselor, parent, or other person who can give you advice.)

4. What are the priorities that result in a happy, content person? Are they part of your life? Do you need to change some priorities?

20 A Blueprint for Your 'Life Purpose'

"If people knew how hard I worked to get my mastery, it wouldn't seem so wonderful at all."
– Michelangelo

If you wanted to build a house, what would you do? Would you walk down the street, turn a corner, and just start building?

No!

Why not?

Because a major project like that takes a lot of planning. First you would have to buy some land and get permission to build. Then you would have to get a contractor, workers, supplies, and so on. You can't just rush into these things.

Well, it's the same thing with your life. You have to plan for success.

What do you want to build? Your life can be:

- A wooden shack

- A straw house

- A teepee

- A pup tent

- A solid brick house.

- A palace

- It's up to you.

Life Building Quiz

Do you have a plan for your life? What does it consist of? Check all of the following statements that are true about you:

____ I know what I am good at doing, and I try to build skills in those areas.

____ I can name three people who are positive influences on my life.

____ My friends help me grow by challenging me to do good for others.

____ I can say no to drugs, alcohol, and sex -- and I do.

____ When others ask my opinion on an important subject, I am not afraid to say what I think and how I feel.

____ When people disagree with me, I understand that that's okay.

____ Before I make a choice, I think about it.

____ When a friend calls, I can say I don't want to go if he has plans to visit a place that would hurt me.

____ Before I go to movies, I make sure I know what they are about and how they are rated. No X- or R-rated movies are shown before my eyes.

____ When older people advise me to do something that is against my morals, I politely refuse.

How many of these did you check?

7-10:   You have most of what you need to build a solid house. You know right from wrong. Start building the house that will suit you best.

4-6:   You have some of the tools you need, but you need a better blueprint. Strengthen your ideas of right and wrong. Learn to develop plans that will help you build a better future.

0-3:   Your toolbox is almost empty. No one can read your plans. Tune in to what is right and wrong. Focus on the principles of this book, and then make plans for a house that will stand. Do you need to gain balance in some areas you've never really thought about? List a few, along with ideas about how you can get balanced. (If you need help, ask a friend, youth counselor, parent, or other person who can give you advice.)

What are the priorities that result in a happy, content person? Are they part of your life? Do you need to change some priorities?

Teens who have their life purposes planned out know how to say no at the right time. They recognize how wrong choices could harm them. When they have a choice, they decide they want a castle, not a shack, so they pick up another building block instead of a broken board.

Let's see how three teens focused on their life purposes and made good choices:

Tony heard that the "whole senior class" would be at a graduation party thrown by another senior. "I won't be there," he told his friend Ben. "Vince runs with a tough crowd. I know he had a party last year that got raided by the police. That kind of party seems like it could be a bad mistake."

Tony was right. One girl had a drug overdose and died the night of the party.

Tony planned ahead to make the right decision. Though he knew that "everyone" was going, he didn't feel as if his life would be short-changed if he missed Vince's party. He wanted better things for his future, and he was willing to plan ahead to have them.

At lunch, Ron's friend Dexter asked if he could look at Ron's paper during the exam they would be having the next period. Ron didn't want to answer right away, so he put Dexter off. All through lunch, Ron worried. He knew what was right, but how could he tell his friend no? Right up until the test started, Ron thought about all the possibilities. He could fail if they were found out; he could get caught, while Dexter got away. But if he didn't do it, his friends might think he was a wimp. They might even cast him aside.

Just before the test, Ron found the courage to say no to his friend. It was not worth the chance of getting a reputation as a cheater, he decided.

Meg wanted to go shopping, but her mother said no.

"You've spent a lot of money this month, and you will need it when you start college. More clothes right now will not pay your bills next September."

When Lee, her best friend, offered to drive to the mall, Meg wanted to go. "Just come and look," Lee suggested. "You don't have to buy anything."

Meg thought about her mother's words. "Nah, if I went, I'd want to spend what I've got. Mom's right-I need to save a little right now. You go on without me."

Having a life purpose takes a lot of planning. If you want to go along and follow the crowd, you don't have to think about it much beforehand. Setting goals and identifying where you want to be will take time, but goals help you have the future you want.

Do you have to have everything in your life tied down in order to have a purpose? No. But you do need to have some ideas about where you are heading.

Setting goals and identifying where you want to be takes time, but goals help you have the future you want.

Plan Ahead

Don't wait until you are at the party and everyone around you is drunk before you decide you should not be there. Don't wait until you are sitting in the back seat and passions flare before you explain your sexual standards. When you are drag racing on the highway, you cannot always know what a car will do. Leaving choices to the last minute almost guarantees mistakes and trouble are coming your way. Setting life purpose goals, and standing up for them ahead of time, will help you do what is right.

Teens who have thought about their life purposes know how to say no at the right time.

Recently, at a conference, I met a senior who was telling younger kids to say no to alcohol. April knows what she's talking about when it comes to drinking and driving. She was in an accident, and her face is scarred. She cannot speak properly. Every day she feels the pain that resulted from one wrong choice. She and her friend waited until it was too late to make the proper decision. Today they regret, but cannot change, what happened, but they can help to keep it from happening to others. So they warn others not to make the same mistake.

When two girls told me of the date rapes they'd suffered from the same boy, it was obvious they'd both waited until too late to say stop. If they had told him up front what their standards were and what they expected from a relationship, this would have given the boy a choice to make. He could respect their wishes or not go on a date with them. He could have avoided a lawsuit the girls brought on him, and all of them would not have the resulting bad memories.

When you only worry about whether or not others will accept you, you run the risk of much pain. You will never see yourself as special if all you're trying to do is live up to the expectations of friends, acquaintances, and classmates. Peer pressure will eat you alive. When you always want to please other people, you cannot choose the right way and make a stand.

Today, satisfying your need to fit in can be relatively easy: you simply go along with the crowd and feel as if you are cool. But who will be with you when you have a sexually transmitted disease, the guilt that comes with an abortion, or a jail sentence for selling drugs? When hard times come, none of the people you tried so hard to impress will hold your hand and help you though your troubles.

You can avoid the pain of all that if you look at your own worth, realize the potential of your future, and aim for it.

Give your life a purpose!

Know Your Own Worth

You are different from everyone else. You have a special package of skills, interests, and situations. No one can do what you can do in life in just the way you can do it.

Maybe you hate history and love science; or you find it hard to stay in class, but can't wait to get out on the hockey field. Neither is right or wrong, it's just you.

Discover the interests and abilities you have been given. Don't try to force yourself into someone else's mold, because it just won't work.

Mission Statements

Lots of businesses have what they call mission statements. In them, businesses define what their goals are and how they plan to reach them. You can have a mission statement for your life -- one that can expand with time. When you write one, you don't have to feel as if you can never add to it, remove an idea from it, or change your message; but having one will help set your sights on something you want to accomplish, and give you a sense of direction.

Frieda described her mission statement with these words: "I want to be the best fiction writer I can be. That means I'll have to spend a lot of time at my computer practicing, take as many English courses as I can, and go to college."

"I want to help people come to know God by serving them," was how Carl defined his goal. "Helping the homeless, feeding the hungry, and training people for work are all practical ways I can reach them as I show them the gospel. When I treat them this way, they will see the Good News in action and will want to know the God I serve."

"I'm good at working with my hands, and I enjoy doing it," Joe explained. "When I fix a car, I want it to run well; and I want the person who owns it to know it's right. My reputation is on the line, so I want people to get only the best."

"When people have seen me, I want them to know they have seen a person with integrity and character," shared Vicky. "If I'm a housewife or an executive, they should still know that. Whether I'm at home or in the workforce, they should see the content of my character coming through."

"I won't be happy if I can't teach," Robert said. "When people's eyes light up and I know they understand how science works, I feel happy. It's what I was meant to do."

All these teens described their mission statements in a few simple words. Each has a future plan that keeps him or her on course. When Frieda doesn't feel like studying, she remembers that she wants to be the best writer ever, and this gives her new energy. When Vicky gets angry, she reminds herself that she isn't living up to her standards. If Robert wants to go to a party and someone offers him a drink, he remembers how that could destroy his brain.

Life purposes are simply larger goals that can help you look into the future. When you need to make plans today, these goals are very helpful in providing guidance.

Focusing on tomorrow gives you a better perspective on the people and ideas around you.

Tiger Woods kept Jack Nicklaus' golf records taped on the wall above his bed as he grew up. He is living proof that having a purpose in life can help keep a person focused on their goals and not on getting into trouble simply because it's popular or easy.

Checkpoints

Review or discuss this chapter using the following questions.

1. What kind of plan for success do you have? How would you describe the "house" you're building?

2. Have you ever said no to something because you saw it would not be good in the long run? What happened? Were you glad you said no?

3. Make a list of all the interests and abilities you feel you have.

4.   Write a mission statement for your life: include where you want to go and how you can get there.

How we act is determined by what we think and what we believe in.

5.   To help you decide what goals you should have, make a list of your interests and abilities. Include the things you do easily and enjoy. Also include the things other people seem to notice about you.

21 The Belief Gap

"People are like stained-glass windows. They sparkle and shine when the sun is out, but when the darkness sets in, their true beauty is reavealed only if there is a light within."
– Elizabeth Kubler Ross

The real basis of the choices we make is the ideas that lie behind them. How we act is determined by the way we really think, the things we believe in. Unfortunately, these aren't always as obvious as they might seem.

"I claimed to have it all together," Nadia said. "People thought that I did. They saw my good grades, all my class activities, and so on. What they didn't know was that Ron and I were having sex regularly.

"I knew it was wrong, but once I got started, it was hard to stop.

"In class I felt as if I were running a race I couldn't get out of. Achieving meant that much to me. My parents wanted me to get into a good college, so they encouraged me to do well in school, take on activities, and so on. I wanted that too, so I aimed high, believing that success would make me happy. The problem was, in all the busyness of my life, I felt lonely. I wanted someone to care just for me.

"I thought Ron did that. When we first had sex, I felt uncomfortable with it, but it also made me feel loved, and I needed that feeling. We kept doing it, despite my doubts.

"On the outside my life said, 'I have it all together; I have a positive attitude and can do what I want.' On the inside it was another matter.

"When Ron and I left for different colleges, we wanted to keep our relationship alive, but we also agreed to give each other the freedom to date others. What I didn't count on was that Ron would find someone else and I wouldn't.

"At Thanksgiving break, Ron told me he didn't want to see me anymore. He'd met a girl at his school, and they were pretty serious.

"'We wanted to get married, didn't we?' I couldn't hold back that cry. 'Do you think I would have had sex with you if I thought we were going to break up?'

"He told me he couldn't ruin both our futures just because we'd had sex. When he said that, I felt my life was already destroyed.

"It's taken me a long time to get back on course after losing Ron, but I have done it. One of the big changes is that I feel better about myself now. I know I don't need sex to have love.

"My parents and I have talked a lot about achievement. They understand that the pressure almost made me nuts, and that I need a balanced life. That includes love from them and time with other people."

Nadia learned that deep down she didn't really believe achievement was her highest goal. Her empty heart kept track: she needed attention from someone. Ron stepped into her life when she was most vulnerable. The short-term gain did not solve Nadia's deeper problem, however.

"I learned that all the external success did not mean I was whole. Inside I felt a lot of doubts about myself. If I had thought more highly of myself, I might have been able to say no to Ron -- and to a lot of pain," Nadia admitted.

When we face choices, we begin to learn what we really believe. How easily we say no to what is wrong and yes to what is right shows what we think of ourselves and what's most important.

Like Nadia, I know what it means to hide behind a mask. As a teen, when I joked around and helped others, I might have seemed as if I really liked people. The problem was that there was one person I didn't think had much value: me.

We can put on masks, hide our own opinions of ourselves and others, and try to avoid the truth about our real beliefs, but sooner or later they will come to the front of our lives.

From Belief to Action

Your actions will often reveal what you actually believe; and similarly, your behavior will be hard to change until you change the belief system that goes with it.

You really can't separate what you believe and what you do. When you believe in something, you take action based on that belief. When you see the results of that action, you feel good or bad about it. If you feel good, you will repeat the action. If you feel bad, hopefully you will try a new belief that will get you out of the cycle.

What happens, however, if you know that you are doing something wrong, but you get feelings of enjoyment from your actions? Unfortunately, you often have to experience enough negatives from your choices to make it seem worthwhile for you to change your beliefs and the habits they cause. You'll also need positive encouragement to make the change.

What Do You Believe?

What you really believe comes out in the person you are, what you enjoy, and the things you do. Though you may try to put on a mask and pretend to the world that you are what you aren't, or even convince yourself you are one thing when you really are another, the truth comes leaking out.

To hear Walt talk, you would think he always makes the right choices. He has an opinion about everything -- how things should be done and who should do them. More often than not he bases his decisions on the idea that he is always right and others are always wrong.

But Walt has a "secret" drinking problem. The problem is that it's only a secret to him. Others have warned him about the effect it could have on his life, but he ignores their efforts. He can't see that he doesn't have his life in order. Though he wants to tell others how to act, he needs to get his own act together first.

Are you like Walt? Do you hide the truth from yourself, while others can plainly see it? That's part of the reason I encourage teens to talk to the people who love them most. Sometimes we need an outside view of where we are going and what we are really like inside. The gentle correction of loving people can help us redirect our lives -- and though it can be painful, it hurts a lot less than the harsh condemnation of those who do not know us well and do not care about our futures.

The gentle correction of loving people can help us redirect our lives.

Belief Discovery Quiz

To discover a few of your inside beliefs, complete the following statements. Where appropriate, fill in more than one answer. Answer honestly, using your whole imagination and your real desires.

1. My greatest success in life is:

2. I feel proudest about this accomplishment:

3. If I could do anything in life, I would:

4. I most enjoy:

5. If I could change anything in my life, it would be:

6. If I could change anything about myself, it would be:

7. When I get mad at myself, it is because:

---

8. I am least proud about (fill in an activity in your life):

9. My greatest need in life is:

How do others see you?

1. When people talk about me, they say:

2. When people tell me I have done wrong, they point out:

3. When people support me, they say:

4. My friends would describe my strongest point as:

5. My friends would describe my weakest point as:

6. My family encourages me to:

7. My family objects that I:

In a short paragraph, describe what you really think and feel about;

1. Your family

2. Other people

3. Your future

Evaluating Your Answers

From these questions, can you see that your actions, the way you think, and the things you enjoy show what you really believe? Your answers describe what is truly important in your life.

When you took the test, did you discover any themes that came up often in the things you enjoy doing, the objections you hear from others, or the positive things they say to you? Have you taken these ideas seriously? Do you really believe in them? Things that come up repeatedly in your life are more likely to be true. For example, when your teachers tell you they see a lot of unused potential in you, it's unlikely that they are all just telling you that to make you feel good. You may not be working up to your best level, and they can see the person you could be if you put more effort into schoolwork.

Be aware of the biases of people, though. "My parents always told me I was 'too religious,'" Julio remarked. "They wanted me to drop out of youth group and stop going to church. They didn't like the church I was going to, and blamed everything I did wrong on my association with it. I talked to my pastor about that, because I didn't want to make a wrong choice.

"When we discussed how my parents felt, my pastor suggested that I try a different tack with them. I'd spent a lot of time telling them about my faith, but I hadn't lived up to those standards.

"Now I try to witness with deeds more than words.

"I've tried to be a responsible son to my parents. Though they don't believe as I do, they no longer tell me not to go to church. In fact they encourage me."

Julio's parents weren't really against his churchgoing. They simply didn't like his dogmatic attitude that was not backed up by loving actions. With his pastor's help, Julio found a way to satisfy both himself and his parents.

Evaluate your own weaknesses, the ideas others have about you, and the future you want to create for yourself. If you need help identifying problem areas, talk to a trusted teacher, pastor, or family member. Explain that you want to discover the beliefs that harm your life, and ask them to gently tell you what they see.

Whatever it takes to stand firm against peer pressure and improve your life, do it!

How to Change Beliefs

Hopefully, you have by now identified the beliefs that harm your life. Maybe some of them have been subtle; or they may have been so obvious you didn't have to think much to find them. Now what can you do to kick them out of your life?

Let's follow Nadia through a plan she used to change her attitudes:

1. *Identify the problem.* Nadia's problem was that deep inside, she felt lonely. For a while, with achievements to keep her busy and with Ron to give her the affection she craved, she was able to hide from the loneliness.

   Losing Ron, however, brought all her isolated, unloved feelings to the surface. "Achieving seemed the way to make people love me. But it entered me into a race I felt I couldn't stop, and I still didn't feel loved."

2. *Identify the thoughts behind the problem.* "The problem was really me. I felt as if people only loved me when I got the best grades, went out for the most activities, and went to the 'right' school. I got caught up in all that; I couldn't see that my value as a person was based not on what I did but on what I was. At heart, I didn't think people could love me for myself."

3. *Identify how your thoughts need to change.* "I had to learn to love myself first," Nadia explained. "Until I did so, nothing else would work. I had to be able to love myself just as I was -- warts and all."

4. *Figure out a plan that will work.* "To love myself I had to learn more about me, who I was, and how to relate to other people. I got rid of a lot of doubts I'd had.

Suddenly I knew who I was, because I started totally accepting myself just as I am. But I had to spend time thinking about the things I did, praying over them, and getting the input of others. That meant spending time with other people, building up a firm social life, and making new friends."

5. *Support a new way of thinking.* "I was so used to thinking I had to do things that it was hard to relax. I had shared my problem with two friends, and they committed to helping me build a better social life. When I started dating again, we set some standards that could help me stand firm. Then I promised to call them and talk over my dates after each one."

6. *Stand firm when troubles come.* "Saying no isn't easy sometimes. I stopped dating one boy who insisted that we have sex, but the peace in my life is worth it. I know there will be other dates. Someday I want to be able to stand before my husband knowing that I waited for him. And now I know that I can do it."

You want to change the beliefs that harm you, and that's the first step. But remember, these beliefs won't change overnight. If you are hiding the truth of your problems or your real emotions from yourself, it may take a while to discover what's actually eating at you. Nadia's real problem wasn't that she was having sex; that was just the way she responded to the problem. Because she did not love herself, she became open to having sex to get the love she needed. Once you have identified the problem, try to deal with it. Perhaps you need to seek out a pastor or counselor, or maybe you simply need to take action. Whatever it takes to stand firm against peer pressure and improve your life, do it!

Reach inside your soul to discover what is important to you. By doing this you discover who you are inside. It helps you believe in yourself and stand up for yourself in this world.

Checkpoints

Review or discuss the chapter using the following questions.

1. Do you have trouble identifying your real beliefs? Why? What can you do about it?

2. Why do people put on masks? Have you ever done this? What was the result?

3. What is the relationship between beliefs and actions? How do feelings – especially, feelings of enjoyment – relate to them?

4. What happens when a person acts one way, but believes something else? How can you avoid that?

5. What did you discover about your beliefs? Were they what you expected, or did you learn something new about yourself? Do you need to make some changes?

22

I Can Make A Difference

"So long as you can sweeten another's pain, life is not in vain."
– Helen Keller

Here are some others who have made a difference:

Julie Leirich works as a cashier at a Los Angeles supermarket. After noticing that good food was being thrown away, she got permission from the store to collect it and take it to feed the homeless. Word got out, and before long, customers wanted to volunteer their time. Eventually, Julie and the others were distributing up to six tons of food a month! Think of how many little children went to bed each night with stomachs full of food instead of eyes full of tears. Julie is proof that one person willing to think of others can truly make a difference.

Ten-year-old Justin Lebo of Saddle Brook, New Jersey, inspired his entire school to think of others instead of just themselves. His heart went out to children in local orphanages. He spent all of his allowance, much of his summer vacation, as well as weekends, fixing up old bikes. Within a couple of years Justin gave away more than 50 bikes! It doesn't take a lot of money or power to affect the lives of others if a person puts their heart and mind to it.

Trevor Ferrell from Gladwyne, Pennsylvania was in 6th grade when he saw a news program of homeless people staying warm by huddling over steam vents in the sidewalks. He asked his dad if people really lived like that. His dad said yes, and that if he wanted to see for himself, he would take Trevor the next day after school.

Almost every night after that, Trevor, along with his parents and his brother or sisters, brought soup, sandwiches, coffee, and blankets to the homeless. He came to know many by name, and they called him "Little Buddy". Three months later the mayor of Philadelphia gave him a special recognition for his nightly visits. He then started asking churches and others to help, and before long, people were bringing piles of clothing and bedding to his front yard. Checks were sent to help in any way possible.

So far, more than 850 volunteers have joined Trevor's concern for the homeless. An old building has been converted into a 50-bed shelter called "Trevor's Place". When Trevor was 15, he addressed the United Nations and met Mother Teresa and President Bush to talk about other ways to help the homeless. This story is just one among many that shows how when one person is filled with compassion for another, it often becomes multiplied by the compassion it inspires in others. You could be the one to start your own chain reaction by thinking of simple ways to reach out to others, right here in your school.

What About You?

Now it's time to put feet to what you have just learned. Please think of some specific act you could perform to make the world, or your school, a better place. Here is a list of suggestions based on what other students have done:

1. Look for a student who is usually seen alone, and introduce yourself to him or her.

2. Smile and make eye contact with people as you pass through the halls.

3. Look around and be aware of people. Are there any who appear sad, hurt, depressed, or empty?

4. Ask your teacher to direct you to those who could use tutoring. Make a difference in their life by investing some of your time. You'll feel great!

5. Think of one good thing about every person you spend time with during the next week.

6. Pick up paper around the school that you didn't drop.

7. Write a positive uplifting note to a teacher who could use some encouragement.

8. Verbally, or even via email, compliment other students for good things you notice about them.

9. Have a positive attitude each day no matter how things are going at home.

10. Refuse to talk negative about anyone for an entire day.

11. Hug a family member and friend every day for the next week.

12. Put a 3x5 card on your mirror, or create a screen saver on your computer, that says "I can make a difference."

13. Walk away from a conversation that is gossiping.

14. Ask for help on your homework from someone you don't know well.

15. Tell a student they did well when he or she gives a report or speech in class.

16. If you are having a difficult time in a relationship at home, make an appointment with that person to discuss the issue.

17. Wish at least 10 people every day for a week to "have a great day".

18. Be nice to your little brother, and in doing so, freak out your mom.

19. Ask your teacher how you could be a better student.

20. Ask someone you don't know well about their interests.

21. Listen twice as much as you talk.

22. Encourage students who ask questions.

23. Don't wait for others to set a good example. Just do it!

24. Give out kindness no matter what you get in return.

25. If you have a problem with someone, go and talk directly with them.

26. Always give others the benefit of the doubt.

27. Treat others the same way you would like them to treat you.

28. Be thankful for school lunches.

29. Be a peacemaker when your friends are arguing..

30. Encourage friends to make up after a fight.

31. Never exclude anyone because of surface stuff like clothes or looks.

32. Strive more to be courageous, not popular.

33. Offer to help with a student who has special needs.

34. Bake some cookies for the office staff.

35. Do at least one helpful thing each day and make sure you don't get caught.

36. Respectfully voice your opinion in class more often.

37. Refuse to yell at anyone.

38. Decide ahead of time to stand up for any student being bullied, laughed at, or ridiculed.

39. Be a shoulder to lean on when someone you know has gotten a bad deal.

40. Develop the habit of saying "good morning" before your teacher does.

41. Write yourself a letter saying how good you feel for trying to make the world a better place.

42. Send your mom flowers for no reason at all.

43. Ignore rude remarks.

44. Laugh at your friend's jokes. Never stop them and say, "Oh I've heard that one."

45. Take your Grandma or Grandpa to lunch.

46. Give your used clothes to someone who could really use them.

47. Donate some time at an elderly care center.

48. Decide to forgive everyone for old grudges.

49. Let your friend win the next game of chess or tennis.

50. Ask someone what his or her dreams are.

51. Consider a different point of view on something today.

52. Tell a friend how much you appreciate them.

53. Smile and wave at teachers when you see them.

54. Join the Big Brothers or Big Sisters when you turn 18.

55. Let another student cut in front of you in the lunch line.

56. Freak people out just by being in a good mood.

57. When you talk with a friend focus totally on them. Don't look around at others.

58. Ask a friend if you can help them solve a problem.

59. Write an encouraging note to a fellow student whose parents are divorcing.

60. When you explain something, do it very patiently.

61. Let everyone know that they can trust you by not spreading rumors or secrets.

62. Refuse to cheat even if your grade will suffer.

63. Find the best teacher in school and ask questions about why he or she became a teacher.

64. Spend some time trying to understand your parents. Keep trying.

65. Share your lunch with a friend.

66. Say, "I respect you too much to argue" instead of raising your voice.

67. Decide to be an optimist all day today.

68. Never send an angry letter.

69. If you forgive someone, never bring it up in the future.

70. Don't demand of others. Ask softly.

71. Become a center of peace.

72. Be genuine.

73. Lift someone's spirits by telling them you are glad they go to your school.

74. Spend more time each day looking for the beauty in others, rather than your hair.

75. Decide today to be against anything evil or hurting.

76. Lighten up a little. Look at the funny side of things.

77. Find a reason to laugh each day.

78. Be contagious in a positive way.

79. Tell a counselor about someone who is depressed and needs help.

80. Never promise to NOT tell on a friend who threatens suicide or shooting someone. If you do make that promise, break it.

81. Take a picture of someone being kind to another.

Procedure:

Circle five statements from the list above that you intend to put into action in your life over the next few days. Fill in the five goals you have selected for yourself.

Everybody matters, and your simple acts and positive attitudes really do make a difference. I am so proud of you for sticking with this book and investing the time necessary to write out these ideas and plans of action. While it can be difficult, these are important steps that assist you in becoming more of the person you deserve to be. You are proving that you can put forth effort today and delay the gratification of simply doing what is both easy and stress free. You are a leader and will make a great mentor to someone else. You are doing what leaders do.

Name: _____

Today's date: _____

By _____ I will do my best to accomplish the following goals:

Example: I will be nice to everyone I pass in the halls.

Example: I am going to ask my teacher whom I can help with tutoring.

1. _____
2. _____
3. _____
4. _____
5. _____

My Second Goal is….
    My 5 steps to achieving this goal are:

Another Goal of mine is…
    My 5 steps to achieving this goal are:

My 4th Goal is…
    My 5 steps are:

My 5th Goal is :
    My 5 steps are:

23 Great Leaders Make Great Mentors

"Treat people as if they were what they ought to be, and you help them to become what they are capable of being."
– *Johann Wolfgang von Goethe*

Do you know what being a mentor is all about? Have you ever had or ever been a mentor? What kind of experience was it?

Have you ever had someone take you under his or her wing, so to speak, and really care about your success in a certain endeavor? That's what mentors do. They walk with you through good times and rough times, offering the benefits of their experience and wisdom.

All of the leadership skills you have been learning in this book are things that will make you an excellent mentor to someone else, if you wish to do it.

Mentoring can be formal or informal. For instance, becoming a big brother through the Big Brothers Big Sisters of America organization is formal, with specific time commitments and rules to follow, and so on. On the other hand, an informal mentor like Rachel Scott, reached out to other students in her Columbine High School that were new, picked on, or had special needs. Being a mentor to someone starts with a desire like the one Rachel had, but goes for a certain period of time: like a senior choosing to meet with a freshman twice a month throughout the year.

Creative Ways To Mentor

Let's take a look at ways in which you could possibly be a lifesaver for a student who might feel like he or she is drowning somewhere in your school.

Would it have been helpful for you, if as a brand new freshman, you had a senior who was interested and committed to making your first year in high school a success? Briefly explain:

Explain how it could have helped you if, before taking certain classes, you had a mentor tell you about different teachers and their style of teaching?

Can you imagine having a mentor who would listen to you when you were having trouble at home, with a certain teacher, or with a friend? Describe a time when such a friend would have meant the world to you.

Mentors care for others and lead by example. They aren't perfect, but they set the standard for their own life a bit higher than most. Below is a list of items that you may want to look over and modify.

Qualities Of A Mentor:

1. *Someone who cares.* Having someone who really cares about you and how you are doing can make a huge difference in a person's life – especially a shy or academically challenged student.

2. *Good listener.* Being there for someone is mostly about listening. We all need to be able to share our feelings and concerns, and the most effective mentors are those who are patient enough to listen. It not only makes the other person feel understood, it gives hope.

3. *Positive outlook on life.* It's very important to have an optimistic outlook on life if you intend on being a leader or mentor in another's life. When things look down and fear sets in, someone who can look on the bright side of things and see a light at the end of the tunnel, is just what the doctor ordered.

4. *Respectful of friends, family, and teachers.* In order to have the respect of the person you are mentoring, you must first give it to others.

5. *Point out the good in others.* Mentors who bring out the best in others are those special leaders who encourage by noticing the efforts of others.

6. *Look for ways to include everyone.* You have what it takes to be an effective guide and encourager of another if you hate to see people left out.

7. *You're willing to ask for help yourself.* No one need handle all of his or her problems alone. It will be hard

to offer help to another if you are uncomfortable in asking for help yourself. Leaders lead by example, especially when it comes to admitting we don't have all of the answers.

8. *Make the effort to contact your mentee twice a month.* There are times when people don't ask for the help they need. You must be willing to make the extra effort to contact your mentee even if only to talk on the phone and ask how things are going.

9. *Confidentiality.* You must be committed to not spread rumors or tell others of your mentee's insecurities. You are a trusted friend and an example that your mentee will hopefully follow someday. Breaking a trust breaks apart lives. **The only time you do not keep something confidential is when someone might get hurt or when someone's life is at stake. Even if it is just "talk", words like "suicide", "shooting", "abuse" are to be taken seriously. You are required to go to your adult leader immediately and tell what you know.**

10. *Show how to have fun without drugs or alcohol.* As we mentioned before, being a leader and mentor is not for everyone. You must be willing to lead by example; and until you can make this commitment, you should refrain from taking on such an important responsibility.

Many Different Ways To Mentor

Becoming a mentor to another student can be a commitment of almost any time limit. Tutoring a student for three weeks in order to pass a final exam would be one example of a very short-term mentoring situation. A more common, long-term mentoring opportunity would be for an older student to take the role of a big brother or big sister to a younger student for the school year.

CREATIVE WAYS TO MENTOR

1. A junior or senior is matched up with a freshman in September, or whatever time of year it is, and helps guide them until the end of the year.

2. A high-school student is matched up with a junior-high student, and meets twice a month throughout the year to listen and give helpful advice.

3. A student, who is good at a certain subject, offers to both tutor another student on that subject and to help teach good study habits for a semester.

4. A high-school student meets with an elementary student who is having trouble getting along with other students. This child may be living with his grandparents, or may be having a really tough time because of a divorce, recent move, or death in the family. By meeting once a week or so, you could be a friend who listens, encourages, and gives hope during a most difficult time.

5. Any student who is good at a given sport can offer to help coach a sport with younger students. You may even get the opportunity to work one-on-one with them.

How to talk to your mentee:

- Help them to not feel embarrassed or uncomfortable by sharing your feelings first. Offer your feelings of what it was like for you as you started high school or didn't make the team.
- Your most important role is that of listener and encourager.
- Try and set up a time where you two can get together at least once every other week.

- Let them know that if they need advice in a hurry, they could call you.
- If your mentee is quiet and shy, have patience and know that it's normal for such a person to be slow at opening up.

What to talk about with your mentee:

Home:

- Ask how things are going.
- Ask if they have ideas of what they could do to make things go better.
- Share what has worked for you.
- Encourage them to develop a relationship with their parents. Offer ways to communicate with parents and earn trust.
- Anything you would like to talk about?

Friends:

- Ask whom are your friends and how are things going?
- What are the things you look for in a friend?
- What could you do to be a better friend?
- Share what is important in getting and keeping good solid friends.

School:

- How are you getting along in your classes?
- What could you do to get better grades?
- Tell me how and when you study. Help them come up with a better plan for preparing for tests if they have none.
- If they are having trouble with a certain class or teacher, discuss ways to make things better. Get advice from your adult leader or another with ideas for coming up with a plan of action for this student to follow.

Congratulate them for successes:

- When they work hard for a good grade send them a note saying how proud you are of them.
- If they were having trouble with detentions and have had two weeks with no trouble take them out for a soft drink. Any little appreciation can make a huge difference in a young person's life especially if they aren't getting any positive support from others.
- Call them to see how they are doing in addition to your meetings. This really shows that someone cares for them and could make all the difference between failure and success.
- Make them feel important by asking their advice on things they are good at. They might be able to offer you ideas in an area like being better organized or a certain skill they are gifted in such as art.

Checkpoints

What are your thoughts on the suggestions you have just read about ways to be a mentor for someone?

Are there any things that you think could be added to the list?

Would you consider being a mentor if your school organized such a program?

What additional training do you feel you would need to do a good job at it?

This is what a school's mentor commitment form might look like:

I want to be a Peer to Peer Mentor. I am willing to invest my time and energy in another person's life.

As a mentor I willingly agree to:

- *Make it a priority to attend as many meetings as possible where encouragement or specific mentor training is offered.*
- *Live by the statements on the Kindness Declaration.*
- *Keep my own emotional support systems (having people I can talk to and receive encouragement and hope from) strong throughout the year.*
- *Put in the disciplined effort needed to keep my grades up.*
- *Keep records of my weekly meetings with my mentees.*
- *Abstain from alcohol, tobacco, and other drugs.*
- *Contact my Adult leader of this program when any problems, questions, or concerns concerning the person I am mentoring as soon as they arise.*
- *I will be committed to support, encourage and help my mentee succeed in school and life. I will not expect them to meet my needs, as I am there to meet theirs.*
- *Come to my Adult leader if I ever hear of anyone talking of suicide, guns, or any mention of any activity where anyone could get hurt.*

Name _____   date _____

Signature _____   phone _____

Note:

These are just suggestions. My goal was to give you a good look at what mentoring is all about. What you do with these suggestions is totally up to you. You may want to meet with a teacher or your principal about becoming a mentor in your school. Check with the school and see if a mentoring program is currently in place, or if one was started in the past but didn't last because of a lack of interest. You could be the person who starts a mentoring program in your school that lasts for years and touches countless lives. Also check with your school to see if they have any good materials available so you won't have to reinvent anything. Contact us at the National Character Education Foundation for more ideas if you would like to pursue this furher, but feel you are at a dead end.

Young people with mentors are:

- 53% less likely to skip school
- 46% less likely to use illegal drugs
- 37% less likely to cut class
- 27% less likely to begin using alcohol
- 33% less likely to hit someone
- 59% experienced improved grades
- 73% of students said their mentors helped raise their dreams, goals, and expectations

(Sources: Big Brothers/Big Sisters of America's 1995 Impact Survey and Louis Harris Poll)

We want to hear about the ways this book has inspired you to be a difference maker. Write us or e-mail us at National Character Education Foundation (www.ncef.net).

24 The Beginning of the Story

"A journey of a thousand miles begins with a single step."
– Lao-tsu, philosopher

Where you go in life will depend largely on the choices you make. It's up to you: you can become the kind of person who makes the right choices and develops good relationships with friends, family, and the community, or you can party today and wallow in regrets tomorrow.

You can become:

- The girl who is in demand for one-night stands, but not for marriage
- The boy who has lost his reputation for honesty, and never tries to earn it back
- The woman who has a child born with deformities because she used drugs in high-school
- The man who is dying of AIDS because he slept around

Or you can become:

- The guy who never has a million dollars, but spends his money wisely
- The girl who has people to support her when times are tough, because she supported them when they needed it
- The woman who has a happy marriage because she said no to sex when she was a teen
- The man who is proud of his work and can support his family without having to become a workaholic

Will you do what is easy -- or what is right? Do you want to feel good about yourself? Or, do you feel ashamed of who you are? Your actions today can start you on a permanent, positive lifestyle.

Every day you have to choose between right and wrong. Do what is right because it is right, because it will benefit you, and because it will enable you to help others.

Who would trade that for all the popularity in the world?

Not until you understand who you are, what you believe, and why you do what you do, will you be able to truly stand up for yourself. Your future can be great. You and your talents have been placed in a certain spot, in a certain family, and in a certain town, to accomplish certain things that only you can do. Unless you stand up for who you are and what is right, you will never achieve what you were put on earth for.

I care about you. While I want you to care deeply about others, I want you to care first and foremost about you. I said it many different ways in this book, but I want to end with this:

You are worth it! You are special! You can become your very best if you remember that it all **starts with you, starting today.**

God bless you.

Your friend,
Bill Sanders

We want to hear about how this book has helped you. Share your story with us or let us help you start a new leadership program in your school.

For information in getting Bill Sanders or other NCEF speakers to your school or conference, contact us at:

www.ncef.net

email Bill Sanders: bill@ncef.net